PROFESSIONAL FOOD AND BEVERAGE
SERVICE MANAGEMENT

PROFESSIONAL FOOD AND BEVERAGE SERVICE MANAGEMENT

Brian Verghese

Head of the Department,
Hindustan Academy of Hotel Management, Bangalore

Macmillan India Limited

First Published 1999
Reprinted 1999

MACMILLAN INDIA LIMITED
Chennai Jaipur Mumbai Patna
Bangalore Bhopal Chandigarh Coimbatore
Cuttack Guwahati Hubli Hyderabad Lucknow
Madurai Nagpur Trivandrum Visahkapatnam
Companies and representatives throughout the world

SBN 0333 93261 7

Published by RAJIV BERI for Macmillan India Limited and
Printed by V N RAO at Macmillan India Press, Chennai 600 041

Acknowledgements

I would like to express my gratitude to the numerous organisations and individuals who gave me assistance and support during the development of this book.

I would like to thank *Mr. Sridhar*, Head of the Food and Beverage Service Department, Institute of Hotel Management, Catering Technology and Applied Nutrition, Bangalore; *Mr. Samuel P Shanthakumar*, Food and Beverage Manager, Le Meridien, Bangalore; *Ms. Anjali Gonsalves*, Training Manager, The Oberoi Towers, Mumbai; *Mr. Kenneth Pinto*, Regional Training Manager, South, Taj Group of Hotels and *Mr. Sukesh Srinivasan*, Head of the Department, Food and Beverage Service Department, K.K.R.M College of Hotel Management, Bangalore. I also express my sincere thanks to *Ms. Prema Menon*, Head of the Department of English, Hindustan Academy of Engineering and Applied Sciences, Bangalore for her patient reading and contribution in improving the manuscript.

I am grateful to the managements of *Le Meridien*, Bangalore; *Taj West End*, Bangalore; *The Oberoi*, Bangalore; *The Capitol*, Bangalore and *The Peacock Restaurant*, Bangalore for their permission to take relevant photographs for their inclusion in the book. I would like to specially mention a word of appreciation for *Mr. Sunil George* who was inspirational in the commencement of this work. I would also like to thank my parents for their support and unstinting encouragement in all projects including this book.

Preface

The aim of this book is to provide a complete guide to the principles, concepts and techniques required for the understanding of operations in the Food and Beverage Service Department. The book has been designed as a comprehensive course book on Food and Beverage Service operations for the students and professionals of the Hotel Management and Catering industry, and takes into account the recent developments and recommendations in syllabi of various examining and awarding bodies as well as the developments in teaching and the hotel industry at large.

Besides covering the knowledge aspects, the book lays a special emphasis on the development of skills needed for the efficient working of the Food and Beverage Service Department. It also highlights the abilities required to translate these skills into effective management practices for the successful functioning of a modern day hotel and restaurant.

Divided into *units* and *chapters,* and supported with exhaustive *glossary, index of terms* and *suggestions for projects,* the book covers all aspects of theory and practicals of Food and Beverage Service. A *brief summary, review questions* and *well conceived relevant projects* are provided along with each chapter to help students and training managers to develop the requisite skills and knowledge to become efficient Food and Beverage Department personnel. The glossary provided in the book gives a clear explanation of terms used in the catering industry and serves as a useful reference to current practices followed in all the outlets of modern day hotels. A large number of accurate illustrations and relevant photographs provided in the book, add depth to the understanding of the subject. Some interesting facts related to the catering industry have been included as snippets of additional information to provide an insight into the origin and cultural aspects of the Food and Beverage Service Department. The useful information given on the operating systems prevailing in the Hotel and Catering industry can serve as a guide in the planning, monitoring and operational functions of all the key personnel in the various outlets of the Food and Beverage Service Department.

In addition to being one of the most relevant textbooks with current information catering to the syllabus requirements of various courses of Hotel Management and Catering, the book is also intended to provide a broad-based support for training personnel in the Food and Beverage Service Department of the Hotel and Catering industry. Thus the book will prove to be a very useful and current training material for students as well as for the personnel serving in the Food and Beverage Service sector.

Contents

UNIT 1

UNIT 2

UNIT 3

UNIT 4

List of figures

Flow charts

An Introduction to the Hotel and Food Service Industry

Objectives : A study of this chapter would enable you to :

✧ *Understand the origin and growth of the hotel and catering industry.*

✧ *Trace the development of the hotel industry.*

✧ *Identify the reasons for its phenomenal growth.*

✧ *Learn about the people who contributed to the development and expansion of the hotel industry.*

Origin — *The Earliest Times*

The hotel industry originated in the 6th century BC and is perhaps one of the oldest commercial endeavours. The earliest inns were just large halls where travellers slept on the floor along with the animals on which they travelled. These conditions prevailed for hundreds of years until the mode of travel changed.

Changes in the mode of transport and travel

The invention of the wheel, one of the greatest events in the history of civilization resulted in the production of quicker modes of conveyance. The speed of travel increased with the development of vehicles. With the advent of the Industrial Revolution in England, travel for business gradually started increasing. A growing economy also led to an increase in travel for recreation and meaningful utilisation of leisure. This created a yearning among people to travel beyond the traditional boundaries.

The era of inns

Travellers of earlier times belonged to different segments of society. They consisted of members of the nobility as well as religious messengers, missionaries, traders and soldiers. Travel for the common man came at a much later date. The aristocrats or nobility travelled on horseback or in carriages, and were usually entertained by people of their own class in castles and mansions of the great estates. They were accommodated and fed, befitting their status, with sumptuous meals and gallons of wine. Monasteries provided shelter to the religious order, while the soldiers were lodged in forts or in tents. It was the traders who helped in promoting the establishment of **inns.** They had no other alternative but to stay in inns for a night or two while travelling.

The improvement of roads and the building of carriages also increased the number of people on the move. To provide accommodation and food for this increasing number of travellers, many types of inns were set up along the frequently travelled roads and pathways. Thus, inn-keeping began its steady growth and became more popular as time progressed.

In earlier times, working in an inn was skill-oriented, and these inns were normally run by a husband and wife team. Inns provided shelter and stabling facilities. Some of them also provided wholesome food, wine and ale.

From Inns to Hotels — *What is a hotel?*

A hotel is defined as a place where a bonafide traveller can receive food and shelter, provided he is in a position to pay for it, and is in a fit condition to be received.

The lead in hoteliering was taken by several nations of Europe, especially France and Switzerland. *Chalets* — small cottages with an overhanging roof found in the Swiss mountains and small hotels, which provided a variety of services, were mainly patronised by the aristocracy of the day.

Around 1760, a type of establishment that became common in Paris, called *Hotel garni* came into vogue. *It was a large house with a number of rooms or apartments, available for rent by the day, week or month.* Its advent signified a more luxurious and organised way of providing lodging, quite different from the basic requirements met by the inns of that period.

The *City Hotel* in New York was the first building meant solely for use as a hotel. It was built in the year 1794. Later, hotels began to be built all over the world. In the year 1827, the **Delmonico brothers,** who were immigrants from Switzerland, opened a pastry shop and café in New York city. It proved to be a change for the better from the eateries of that era, and led to the opening of their first restaurant

Fig. 1.1 *The City Hotel at New York in the year 1794*

a few years later. Thus, the art of food service became recognised as an important part of the dining experience.

The concept of chain hotels — *A big boom*

The big boom in the hotel industry came in the 1920s, when the concept of chain hotels was born, under the stewardship of **E.M. Statler.** However, during the Great Depression of the 1930s, there was a considerable decrease in business thereby affecting the growth

> **For interest**
> *The first roadside inn to be called a motel in the 1920s was the Motel Inn in San Luis Obispo, California, the USA.*

of the hotel industry. Immediately after the Second World War, the hotel industry regained its prominence and registered a steady growth. Of late, there has been a phenomenal growth in the hotel industry, particularly in those countries which attract business travellers and tourists in large numbers from all over the world. In the 1950s, *Motels* and *International hotel chains* gave a big boost to the industry. These chains either bought up smaller individually owned properties, or built their own hotels. Many individual hotel operators merged with these international hotel chains, as it increased their ability to cope with the growing competition.

International hotel chains — *How did they function?*

International hotel chains provided the following options to individual hotel owners.

- *Partnership*

Sharing of profit and equity.

- *Franchise*

Giving a brand name to a franchisee, and helping to market the hotel, in return for franchise and marketing fees.

- *Management*

Managing the hotel in exchange for management fees and a share in the profits, known as incentive fees.

- *Leasing*

Lease means the taking over of all operational aspects of the property for a specific period of time, paying the lease either as a fixed sum or as a percentage of turnover.

Growth of the hotel industry

The expansion of cities all over the world and their rapid growth led to further development of the travel and hospitality industry. Restaurants of all kinds and hotels of various sizes and types mushroomed and the customer became used to a standardised type of service. Based on this standardisation, the hotel industry felt the need for trained hoteliers and skilled professionals to manage the various establishments and provide services set to a predetermined standard.

As the demand for skilled professionals in all departments of a hotel increased, the need was felt for specialised training institutions. Today the level of training in the catering industry is highly advanced and specialised.

Specialised dining

As far as specialised dining was concerned, it was **César Ritz** and **Auguste Escoffier,** who popularised public dining in Europe. Gradually dining out became fashionable. The pioneers in this field set very exacting standards, with superb cuisine and impeccable and stylish service of food and wine. By the turn of the century, they had taken London by storm and given Londoners a new fad — *a gracious dining experience.*

Expansion in the food and beverage services

With the increase in affluence among many segments of society, public dining gained greater acceptance and led to expansion and changes in the food and beverage services to suit varied tastes.

John Naisbitt predicted that as industrial societies came to progressively bank on those who provide service and information, there would be an unprecedented diversity in the hotel industry and that ethnic and speciality restaurants would spring up to satisfy the consumer. He also predicted that by the end of the 20th century, all types of catering would lay stress on giving to the consumer what he would like, within the limits set by each establishment. The personnel would be professionally trained, and every establishment would try to satisfy its clients in all aspects of the dining experience, be it through perfectly presented delicious food, unobtrusive and stylish service or elegant ambience.

Modern day hotels are all that and much more : *a city within a city*. With the use of both modern technology and the very best of what professionally trained hotel personnel can offer, the service provided to a guest is both courteous and gracious.

SUMMARY

1. The hotel industry is one of the oldest commercial endeavours.
2. Inns in earlier times provided only basic facilities and were normally run by a husband and wife team.
3. The Delmonico brothers were pioneers in the food and beverage industry.
4. E.M. Statler introduced the concept of chain hotels.
5. César Ritz and Auguste Escoffier were the first to popularise public dining in Europe.
6. John Naisbitt predicted the advent of ethnic and speciality restaurants with professionally trained personnel to satisfy the consumer.
7. Modern day hotels with latest technology and specialised personnel provide guests with courteous and efficient service.

Review Questions

Answer the following questions :

1. Explain the origin of the hotel industry.
2. The invention of the wheel is seen as one of the greatest events in the progress of the hotel industry. Discuss.

3. In the past only selected segments of the population used to travel. Describe the various types of accommodation that were available for their use.

4. List the most important features stressed in a modern hotel.

5. Explain the options international hotel chains offer to individual hotel owners.

6. Define the following :

   (i) A hotel   (ii) Hotel *garni*   (iii) A chalet

7. Describe what is meant by specialised dining.

Projects

1. *List the names and addresses of some franchise hotel properties in India.*

2. *Explain the significance of the term franchise in the context of the contract that governs the business relations between the contracting parties.*

3. *Trace the development of the hotel industry in India.*

Glossary

Auguste Escoffier : The most famous French chef, known as the *emperor of chefs.*

Catering : Providing the service of food and beverage.

César Ritz : A famous Swiss hotelier, founder of the Ritz hotels at London and Paris.

Chain hotels : A group of hotels belonging to the same company.

Cuisine : A style or method of cooking. It also means kitchen in French.

Delmonico brothers : Immigrants to the USA from Switzerland. They opened a pastry shop and café in 1827 in New York city.

E.M. Statler : The originator of the concept of chain hotels.

Franchise : The license granted by a company to use its name for a fee.

Inn : A house providing food, beverage and accommodation.

Motel : A hotel on a highway, with individual parking space near each room.

Nobility : A segment of society, belonging to a high social class.

Stabling facilities : The facility to house and care for horses.

2

Classification of Food and Beverage Service Facilities
∎∎∎∎∎∎∎∎∎∎∎∎∎∎∎∎∎∎∎∎∎∎∎∎∎∎∎∎

> **Objectives :** A study of this chapter would enable you to :
> ✧ *Describe a catering establishment.*
> ✧ *List the various types of catering establishments.*
> ✧ *Understand the difference between primary and secondary catering.*
> ✧ *Identify and differentiate between the vast array of currently existing catering establishments.*

What is a catering establishment?

An organisation that provides food and beverage is called a **catering establishment.** There are a number of ways of classifying food and beverage operations in today's catering field. There are *primary* catering establishments and *secondary* catering establishments.

Primary catering establishments

Establishments such as *hotels, restaurants* and *fast food* outlets which are primarily concerned with the provision of food and beverage are called **primary catering establishments.**

Secondary catering establishments

In **secondary catering establishments,** the provision of food and beverage is a part of another business such as *welfare catering* and *industrial catering.*

Catering establishments are usually classified on the basis of the demands being met by them. The main aim of any catering organisation is to attract different sections of the public to use its facilities, keeping in view the price of food and service it offers in relation to the location of the property and the class of clientele it attracts.

The food and beverage sector

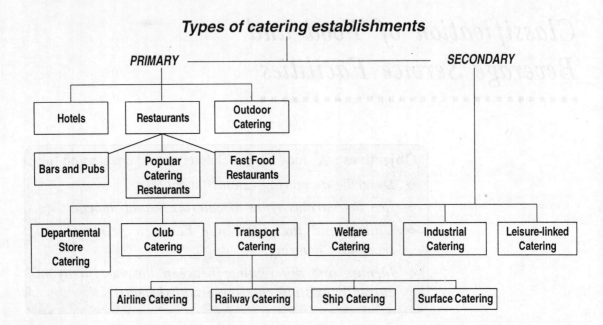

Types of catering establishments

Hotels

The main purpose of hotels is to provide accommodation, which may or may not include the service of food and beverage. A hotel may be a small family-run unit providing a limited service in one restaurant, or a large luxury hotel providing service through a number of outlets such as the *coffee shop, room service, banquets, speciality restaurant, grill room* and *cocktail bars*. The service in these types of hotels is usually personalised and the tariff is very high, as they generally cater to persons of a high social standing. Medium class hotels are similar to luxury hotels, though their surroundings are less luxurious and the facilities are not of the same standard as those available in the luxury category. The prices in the various categories of hotels, often depend upon the service and choice of food and beverage that they offer to their clientele.

Restaurants

Restaurants are of different standards. A **speciality** or an **A grade** restaurant's objective is the provision of food and beverage. The food, service and prices are often comparable to those of similar restaurants in luxury hotels. They offer a wide choice from an elaborate menu and a very high quality of service.

Fig. 2.1 *A 'speciality' or an 'A grade' restaurant*

Bars and pubs

The idea of **pubs** is fairly new in India. It has been borrowed from the concept of *public houses* in England and adapted to Indian conditions. They are geared to provide service of all types of alcohol with an emphasis on draught beer and good music. Food may also be served from a limited menu.

Popular catering restaurants

The objective of popular catering restaurants is to provide a quick and economical meal, in a clean and standardised dining room. These restaurants are commonly used by the vast urban population of India. They are of various styles and categories. Some restaurants serve only vegetarian food while some specialise in the food of a particular region such as the *Punjab* or *Andhra*. Some restaurants serve food from more than one region.

The entry of *pizza* parlours and westernised popular food into India provides the urban Indian a wider choice, in the types of popular restaurants to choose from. The numerous outlets that have sprung up all over the country in the last decade, show a new trend in the urban citizen's eating habits. This has resulted in an increased awareness among the public about the availability of various types of cuisine and catering services.

Fast food restaurants

There is a predominant American influence in fast food style of catering. The service of food and beverages in a fast food restaurant is at a faster pace, than at an *a la carte restaurant* as the menu is compiled with a special emphasis on the speed of preparation and service. To make this type of service financially viable, a large turnover of customers is necessary. The investment is rather large, due to the specialised and expensive equipment needed and high labour costs involved.

Fig. 2.2 *A fast food outlet*

Outdoor catering

This means catering to a large number of people at a venue of their choice. Hotels, restaurants and catering contractors meet this growing demand. The type of food and set up depends entirely on the price agreed upon. Outdoor catering includes catering for functions such as marriages, parties and conventions.

Departmental store catering

Some departmental stores, apart from carrying on their primary activity of retailing their own wares, provide catering as an additional facility. This type of catering evolved when large departmental stores wished to provide food and beverages to their customers as a part of their retailing concept. It is inconvenient and time consuming for customers to take a break from shopping, and have some refreshments at a different location. Thus arose the need for some sort of a dining facility in the departmental store itself. This style of catering is becoming more popular and varied nowadays.

Club catering

This refers to the provision of food and beverages to a restricted clientele. The origin of this service can be traced back to England, where membership of a club was considered prestigious. Today, in India there is a proliferation of clubs to suit different needs. Clubs for people with similar interests such as *turf clubs*, *golf clubs* and *cricket clubs*, to name a few, have sprung up. The service and food in these clubs tend to be of a fairly good standard and are economically priced.

Night clubs are usually situated in large cities that have an affluent urban population. They offer entertainment with good food and expensive drinks.

Transport catering

The provision of food and beverages *to passengers, before, during and after a journey* on trains, aircraft, ships and in buses or private vehicles is termed as transport catering. These services may also be utilised by the general public, who are in the vicinity of a transport catering unit.

The major forms of modern day transport catering are *airline catering, railway catering, ship catering* and *surface catering* in coaches or buses which operate on long distance routes.

Airline catering

Catering to airline passengers on flights, as well as at restaurants situated at airports is termed as airline catering. Modern airports have a variety of food and beverage outlets to cater to the increasing number of air passengers. Catering to passengers en route is normally contracted out to a flight catering unit of a reputed hotel or to a catering contractor.

Railway catering

Catering to railway passengers both during the journey as well as during halts at different railway stations, is called railway catering. Travelling by train for long distances can be very tiring, hence a constant supply of a variety of refreshment choices helps to make the journey less tedious.

Ship catering

Voyages by sea were once a very popular mode of travelling, but with the onset of air travel, sea voyages have declined sharply. However, recently, it has again become popular with a large number of people opting for pleasure cruises. Both cargo and passenger ships have kitchens and restaurants on board. The quality of food, service and facilities offered depends on the class of the ship and the price the passengers are willing to pay.

There are cruises to suit every pocket. There are cruises of two to five days duration which offer budget accommodation comparable to a limited service hotel, while luxury cruises of seven days to three months duration offer luxurious staterooms and various other facilities that are comparable to a first class resort. Luxury cruises pamper travellers with deluxe accommodation and attentive and specialised service at a very high premium.

All these ships provide a variety of food and beverage service outlets, to cater to the individual needs of the passengers. They range from room service and cocktail bars to speciality dining restaurants. The ships that cater to the cruise sector today, are virtually floating palaces with every conceivable guest service available aboard them.

This sector has been growing in popularity in recent times, and has become affordable to a large cross-section of people. Cruise companies offer attractive packages to passengers. To provide these services, a considerable demand for professionally trained manpower has been created.

Surface catering

Catering to passengers travelling by surface transport such as buses and private vehicles is called surface catering. These eating establishments are normally located around a bus terminus or on highways. They may be either government run restaurants, or privately owned establishments. Of late there has been a growing popularity of *Punjabi* style eateries called *dhabas* on the highways.

Welfare catering

The provision of food and beverages to people to *fulfil a social need, determined by a recognised authority,* is known as welfare catering. This grew out of the welfare state concept, prevalent in western countries. It includes catering in hospitals, schools, colleges, the armed forces and prisons.

Industrial catering

The provision of food and beverages to people *at work, in industries and factories at highly subsidised rates* is called industrial catering. It is based on the assumption that *better fed employees are happy and more productive.* Today, labour unions insist on provision of this facility to employees.

Catering for a large workforce may be undertaken by the management itself, or may be contracted out to professional caterers. Depending on the choice of the menu suggested by the management, catering contractors undertake to feed the workforce for a fixed period of time at a predetermined price.

Leisure-linked catering

This type of catering refers to the provision of food and beverages to people engaged in leisure. The increase in leisure and a large disposable income for leisure activities has made it a very profitable form of catering. This includes the provision of food and beverages through different *stalls* and *kiosks* at *exhibitions, theme parks, galleries* and *theatres.*

SUMMARY

1. Various catering establishments are categorised by the nature of the demands they meet.

2. The main purpose of a hotel is to provide accommodation with or without food and beverage service.

3. Fast food restaurants are mainly characterised by a large turnover of customers and speed of preparation and service.

4. Transport catering provides food and beverage services to passengers travelling by air, sea, rail and surface transport.

5. Catering to people is undertaken in a wide range of establishments such as restaurants, pubs, clubs and fast food outlets.

Review Questions

Answer the following questions :

1. What is a catering establishment?

2. How are catering establishments classified?

3. Describe the following :
   i. Popular catering
   ii. Outdoor catering
   iii. Welfare catering
   iv. Industrial catering

4. What do you understand by the term *fast food* ? Name a few fast food restaurants located in your city.

5. What is leisure-linked catering?

6. Explain the different types of transport catering available in India.

Projects

1. *Research and document the functioning of a fast food outlet in India and its intended market.*

2. *Establish how transport catering is different from catering in the outlets of a hotel.*

Glossary

Catering contractor : Catering professionals who undertake to provide food for a fixed period of time at a set price.

Dhabas : *Punjabi* style eateries, found on the highways of India and in towns of North India.

Draught beer : Beer which is stored and served from a barrel or a cask.

Fast food outlet : A place where speed of preparation and service of food is emphasised.

Industrial catering : Preparation and service of food for employees working in factories at subsidised rates.

Package holidays : A holiday package in which accommodation, travel and sometimes all meals are included in the price and is paid for in advance by the customer.

Primary catering : Establishments which are primarily concerned with the service of food and beverages.

Pub : Short for *public house.* A place where beer and spirits are served.

Restaurant : A place where food is prepared and served to guests for a price.

Secondary catering : The provision of food and beverages is a part of another business.

Stateroom : A private cabin on a passenger ship.

3

The Food and Beverage Service Department

Objectives : A study of this chapter would enable you to :
- *Understand how the food and beverage service department is organised.*
- *Identify the operational areas in the food and beverage service department.*
- *Learn the functions of different outlets, and how they meet the demands of customers.*
- *Comprehend various operating systems and policies of different outlets and their importance.*

Outlets in a food and beverage service department

The food and beverage service department of a hotel is the most labour intensive department. It is divided into sections called *outlets* for effective management and control. Each outlet is headed by an *outlet manager* and has its own operational procedures. The food and beverage manager delegates authority and responsibilities to the outlet managers. Teamwork is the essence of a well-run food and beverage service department.

The various outlets in a food and beverage service department of a five star hotel are as follows.

Banquets

This outlet is usually the **largest revenue earning** outlet in the food and beverage service department. It serves food and beverages to a gathering of people at special functions such as weddings, parties, receptions, cocktail dinners, seminars, conferences and meetings. Banquet functions can be held at lunch or dinner time and the pattern of operations may vary from one kind to another. The outlet also rents out *banquet halls* for exhibitions, concerts and other programmes.

The history of banqueting

The history of banqueting was not recorded in detail until the Middle Ages. The modern banqueting menu is said to have originated during the medieval period. The late 18th and 19th centuries saw many revisions of the menu. The three primary courses with multiple dishes were transformed into a series of nine courses, each featuring an individual item. The French cuisines and menu formats, threaded their way through the colonies via English recipes and customs. Records tracing the development of the banquet menu through the centuries, provide a rich and exciting chronicle of food items, recipes and traditions.

> ### For interest
> *It is believed that banqueting has its roots in the traditions of the Greeks and the Romans, who developed a banquet feast consisting of twenty-five courses. The twenty-five courses eventually evolved into three, each course in turn offering as many as twenty-five dishes.*

The Indian banqueting menu

The Indian banqueting menu consists of a fixed or predetermined buffet menu selected from the varied cuisines of India, or a selection of dishes from Continental food.

Organising a banquet function

Banquet functions are normally planned in advance, since considerable time is required for planning and organising a function. However, the food and beverage service personnel should be prepared for any exigency as guests may suddenly demand the unexpected.

The banquet outlet has its own staff who work in shifts to cater to these functions. The banquet sales assistants are responsible for managing the banquet reservation system in the banquet office.

The duties of the banquet sales assistants include :

- Taking bookings for all functions to be held in the hotel.

- Preparing the *Function Prospectus* (FP) or *Banquet Function Contract* (BFC) that contains all the details of the proposed function according to the guest's wishes.

- Coordinating with the banquet operational staff to ensure that the function is planned according to the details specified in the Function Prospectus.

Pricing for these events is worked out on the basis of the estimated costs and the policy of the concerned organisation.

Fig. 3.1 *Conference hall set-up for banquets*

HOTEL XYZ XXXUUUIIVV	Function Prospectus	No. 121

DATE	DAY	FUNCTION	VENUE	NO. OF PERSONS Min _____ Max _____	TIME From _____ to _____

Name of the Party _____

Contact Person _____

Address _____

_____

☎ *Off.* _____   *Res.* _____

Fax _____   *Others* _____

Rate :   Food _____   Beverage _____

Vegetarian ☐   Non-Vegetarian ☐

MENU

Food Service _____   Pick up Time _____

REQUIREMENTS FOR THE FUNCTION

White board ☐   OH Projector ☐   Flip Chart ☐

Screen ☐   Podium ☐   T.V/V.C.R ☐

Computer ☐   Mikes ☐

Pads/Pencils _____   Special request _____

Floral Arrangements:

Small _____   Medium _____

Large _____   Bud vase _____

BILLING:

Advance Rs. _____   R. No. _____   Dt. _____

1. I agree to abide by the rules of the hotel.
2. All disputes are subject to Indian Laws and XXXUUUIIVV courts alone shall have jurisdiction to try such disputes.
3. The hotel is not responsible for safety of any valuables left in the banquet hall.
4. I agree to pay for either the guaranteed number or the actual plate count whichever is higher.

Date : _____

Banquet Manager : _____   Signature of the guest : _____

MISCELLANEOUS

Photographer _____   Music _____

Lighting _____   Others _____

FUNCTION SIGNAGE

SEATING ARRANGEMENTS

CC : GM/FC/CHEF/F&BCC/ACCTS/HK/KIT STEW/SALES/BQTS/FILE

Fig. 3.2 *A function prospectus*

Since no two events or functions are similar, additional information of the event/function may have to be collected. It is very important that a responsible person checks all the details before the event/function commences. Preparing a checklist of various arrangements that have to be made before the event or function, may be very useful. Table set-up, beverage arrangements, the menu, and all other relevant details should be worked out several days in advance and checked thoroughly on the day of the function.

A Banquet Captain's Checklist

Function_____ Date_____ No. of persons____

Time

Function starts at _____   Finishes at _____
Meal to be served first?   ☐
Reception to be held first?   ☐

Control

Entry by invitation ☐   Sale of tickets ☐
Staff to check invitations/tickets?   Yes ☐ No ☐

If yes, specify the arrangements made _____
_____

Signages

Are signages necessary?   Yes ☐ No ☐
Checked by?   _____

Beverages

Beverages to be served :   Yes ☐ No ☐
To be served at the same venue? Yes ☐ No ☐
If no, specify venue _____
Special instructions from the host on service, if any?
_____

Floral arrangements

Nos. : _____ Small ☐ Medium ☐ Large ☐
Location of floral arrangements. _____

Gifts

Gifts/bouquets/garlands to be arranged? Yes☐ No☐

Music

Is music to be arranged?   Yes ☐ No ☐

Type of music : Band ☐   Piped music ☐
Have arrangements been
made and space allocated?   Yes ☐ No ☐

Amplification

Microphones Nos. : _____ Speakers Nos.: _____
Location _____. Equipment checked? Yes ☐ No ☐

Photographer/Videographer

Should the hotel arrange for a
photographer/videographer?   Yes ☐ No ☐
If yes, has the photographer/
videographer been contacted?   Yes ☐ No ☐

Name and address of the photographer/videographer arranged to cover the event.

_____   _____
_____   _____

Phone _____   Phone _____

Hall set-up and table plan

Hall set according to
the client's wishes?   Yes ☐ No ☐
Type of table plan :   Formal ☐ Informal ☐
Is there enough aisle
space for movement?   Yes ☐ No ☐

Master of ceremonies

Master of ceremonies?   Yes ☐ No ☐
Should the hotel arrange?   Yes ☐ No ☐
If there are speeches, when will they take place:
before the meal/during the meal/after the meal

During speeches, should waiters :
Leave the room   ☐   Continue service ☐

Permits or licenses

Any special permits necessary?   Yes ☐ No ☐
Have they been obtained?   Yes ☐ No ☐

Engineering

Extra power needed?   Yes ☐ No ☐
Special lighting requested?   Yes ☐ No ☐
Has it been arranged?   Yes ☐ No ☐
Standby in case of power failure? Yes ☐ No ☐

Arrival and departure

Entrance to be used. _____
Parking attendants. Nos. _____
Has security been informed?   Yes ☐ No ☐

Fig. 3.3 *A banquet captain's checklist*

Coffee shop

This outlet is *open twenty-four hours* for service. It generally serves **pre-plated food.** However, in the case of Indian food, the *entrée* dishes are placed on the table and the service is not very elaborate and formal.

Promptness of service is of prime importance. The prices are not as high as in a

Fig. 3.4 *A coffee shop*

speciality restaurant. Dining in a coffee shop is a casual affair, and many coffee shops have a list of enthusiastic regulars. Coffee shops in luxury hotels are often the only venues where one can get a decent meal or a snack long after other restaurants have closed. Liquor is not served after licensing hours; however, this depends on the laws of the State.

The menu in a coffee shop is varied. Different menus are used during different times of the day/night, for example, there is normally a breakfast menu, a lunch and dinner menu, a snack menu and a midnight menu. The number and types of menus are decided by the management in consultation with the chef and the food and beverage manager after carefully studying the market conditions, the location of the hotel and the availability of staff to man the coffee shop round the clock.

The revenue generated from this outlet is the second highest in the food and beverage service department. It is however necessary to change the menu, decor and ambience from time to time to keep the guests coming back. This outlet is also the venue for many food festivals.

Speciality restaurant

Service in a speciality restaurant is both *formal and stylish.* The prices tend to be high because of higher overheads. The menu may be an *a la carte,* buffet, or a *table d'hôte.* Waiters should be highly skilled, as specialised services such as preparation of food at tables and *flambés,* may have to be done.

Normally every five star hotel has at least one speciality restaurant. In India, multi-cuisine speciality restaurants are fairly popular, as they offer guests a wide variety of choice of food items. These restaurants normally function during lunch and dinner sessions and at times are open only for dinner. Entertainment in the form of music by a band or an orchestra may also be provided. If it is an ethnic restaurant, traditional dances may also be performed.

For a speciality restaurant to be profitable, it should provide not only *excellent food* and *service* but also good *decor* and *ambience*. Hence care should be taken to enhance the decor and ambience of the restaurant. The equipment used should be of a high standard as this will enrich the entire dining experience of guests.

Fig. 3.5 *A table at a speciality restaurant*

Room service

This outlet is an *integral part* of the food and beverage service department. It has a small turnover in terms of revenue, but a great deal of effort and labour is necessary to run this outlet. It is regarded as a guest facility, and is functional round the clock in all luxury hotels. The menu is often a simplified version of what is available in the coffee shop, with prices slightly higher to compensate for the higher overheads in terms of staff and equipment.

Fig. 3.6 *A room service tray set for lunch*

Accuracy and *promptness* are of utmost importance in a room service outlet. An efficient room service outlet is one that can carry out an order *accurately* and within a *specified time*. The room service tray or trolley should be checked by the duty captain and the waiter before it is taken to the guest. This ensures that the waiter takes the relevant food ordered by the guest along with the necessary cover and accompaniments. There is normally an average waiting time for each set of orders, which may differ from hotel to hotel depending upon the infrastructural facilities.

If there is a delay, the guest should be informed immediately, and efforts should be made to see that the order reaches the guest as soon as possible. To speed up orders, specially during peak hours, some hotels have floor pantries.

Clearance is one of the main indicators of efficiency of a room service outlet. One of the major responsibilities of this outlet is to ensure that all trays and trolleys are cleared from guest rooms after the service is done. Pilferage and breakage of equipment can also be avoided by quick clearance. A strict vigil should be maintained by the duty captain to follow up clearance by the staff. There is nothing more annoying to a guest than the sight of used trays and trolleys in the corridors.

The room service outlet is also responsible for the placement of food and beverage amenities for regular guests and VIP's. The amenities may include fresh fruit, cookies, dry fruits and nuts and a soft bar or a hard liquor bar.

To personalise service to their guests, most luxury hotels offer *valet service* or *butler service*. If such a service is a part of the facility on offer, then the room service outlet oversees and monitors this service also. Since this service is associated with class and finesse, the valets or butlers should be trained in the fine art of taking care of all the needs of the guests. They should be able to coordinate with the other departments of the hotel such as housekeeping, front office, food and beverage service and the kitchen.

Good service in this outlet is usually rewarded with a substantial tip. If a tip is given, the guest should be thanked politely. One should not solicit tips.

Bar

There are normally two kinds of bars in Indian hotels. One is the **public** bar and the other is the **service** or **dispense** bar. The public bar is located in the public area, and is used for the service of paying customers, be it in-house guests or non-residents. Cocktail snacks may also be served here. Service should be fast and discreet and the bar staff should be well prepared to handle the rush hour. Good decor, ambience, efficient staff and availability of a wide variety of beverages and snacks help to attract more customers.

The service or the dispense bar is used for dispensing drinks to other outlets of the hotel such as coffee shop, room service outlet, banquets and the speciality restaurant. It is generally located in the back area of the hotel and is open round the clock. It should be adequately equipped to meet the demands of all the outlets.

Barbecue restaurant

This is an optional outlet generally located near a swimming pool. Of late, such restaurants have become popular, especially during summer.

For interest
The term barbecue is said to have originated from the ancient French practice of cooking the whole animal over an open fire. In French 'barbe' means beard and refers to the whiskers of the animal and 'queue' means the tail.

During the day, the space is used by sunbathers, and in the evenings it is used for private functions, or as a barbecue restaurant for *a la carte* guests. This is primarily done to increase the revenue of the hotel as well as to provide guests with another venue to dine. The food served in this outlet is barbecued over a charcoal grill.

Pastry or baker's shop

This outlet has become very popular in Indian luxury hotels during the last few years. It caters to both in-house and non-resident guests. It may be a self service counter, or a small area where there are a few tables with waiter service. It is normally located in the lobby area of the hotel. Most of the business in this outlet is in the form of take-aways.

SUMMARY

1. The food and beverage service department is divided into different outlets. They are banquets, coffee shop, speciality restaurants, bar, room service, barbecue restaurants and pastry shop.

2. Each outlet has its own operating system and functions and is headed by an outlet manager.

3. The banquet outlet is the largest revenue earning outlet in the food and beverage service department.

4. Coffee shop and room service outlets are twenty-four hour service outlets.

5. Speciality restaurants offer guests a wide variety of choice of food and beverages.

6. There are two types of bars in hotels namely the main or public bar and the service or dispense bar.

7. Some hotels also have a poolside barbecue restaurant and a pastry or a baker's shop.

Review Questions

Answer the following questions :

1. What are the main things that a banquet captain should check before a function/event commences?

2. What are the attributes of an efficient room service outlet in a hotel?

3. Why is a coffee shop normally a busy outlet?

4. Explain what is meant by a speciality restaurant.

5. Describe the different types of bars in a hotel and list the differences in the operating system of each.

6. Explain why the food and beverage service department is the most labour intensive department in a hotel.

Projects

1. *Draw a chart showing the different outlets of the food and beverage service department and describe the differences in their styles of functioning.*

2. *Illustrate with examples the common goal of all the outlets in the food and beverage service department.*

Glossary

Amenities : The different eatables that a hotel places in a guest's room on a complimentary basis, for example, fruits, nuts and cookies.

Banquet : An outlet that caters to the service of food and beverage to a large gathering of people.

Banquet Function Contract or Function Prospectus : A contract entered into between a guest and the banquet outlet, mentioning all the details of the function/event.

Bar : An outlet that primarily serves alcoholic beverages.

Butler/valet : A highly trained member of the staff who takes care of all the needs of a resident guest.

Ethnic restaurant : A restaurant serving non-European food such as Indian, Chinese or Polynesian.

Multi-cuisine : A restaurant that serves food from different countries such as Indian, Chinese and Continental.

Outlet : A section in the food and beverage service department.

Poolside barbecue : An outlet by the swimming pool that specialises in food cooked over a charcoal grill.

Speciality restaurant : A fine dining outlet in which service is both formal and stylish.

Table plan : A written plan for seating arrangements in a restaurant or a banquet hall.

4

Supervision and Organisational Hierarchy

■ ■

> **Objectives :** A study of this chapter will enable you to :
>
> ✧ *Identify the role of a supervisor in relation to all the outlets.*
>
> ✧ *Describe the functions of the key personnel of the department.*
>
> ✧ *List and discuss the hierarchy of the food and beverage service department and the role its key personnel play in its functioning and organisation.*

Supervision means to oversee the actions or work of a person. High on the list of factors that make employees happy in their jobs, is the attitude of the supervisor towards them. An employee considers the supervisor as a part of the management, and the management in turn considers the supervisor as one who represents the working force. An efficient supervisor should be able to maintain a *healthy relationship* with his seniors, colleagues, subordinates and guests. He should be able to *interpret the policies of the organisation, train workers and direct procedures to achieve positive results.*

Qualities of a supervisor

Personality traits

An efficient supervisor should :

- possess a pleasing personality and good temperament
- be a person of high integrity
- have the ability to think independently and profit by experience
- be able to judge things objectively
- be honest and loyal to the organisation
- have good health, good manners and emotional stability

Work related attitudes

Expertise

A supervisor should be alert, punctual and systematic. He should have the technical expertise to recognise a job properly done and to enhance the performance of the team. This gives the employees a sense of security and well being and instils in them a sense of self-confidence to perform better.

Communication and goal setting

A supervisor should be able to communicate his instructions clearly to every employee. He should set realistic goals in consultation with the employees so that they own these goals and work hard to achieve them.

Delegation

A supervisor should know when and how to delegate authority. *Delegation means the entrustment of responsibility and authority to another person to perform a task.* Proper delegation of work to subordinates will not only aid in their professional development but also leave the supervisor with enough time to do more important tasks that may not be possible to delegate. However, it should be noted that delegation is most successful in a climate of mutual confidence.

The following factors should be taken into consideration in determining the extent of delegation necessary in a specific organisation.

Cost : Before delegating the work, a supervisor should take into account the cost factor. He should ascertain if any saving in terms of time, manpower and money is possible by delegating work to a subordinate. He should also consider the losses the organisation may incur if the task is badly performed.

Competence : A supervisor should carefully assess the competence and experience of the subordinate while delegating the work. The extent of delegation should depend on the capability of the subordinate.

Control system : A supervisor should ascertain whether the organisation has a proper system of evaluating the gains achieved as a result of delegation of work. He should find out if there are possibilities of undoing the harm that the delegation may cause.

Key personnel

The food and beverage service department usually has the largest staff. Able leadership and supervision is required to effectively direct the department and guide the staff.

The personnel in the food and beverage service industry require practical knowledge of operations as even a small error can cause displeasure to the guest. Coordination of activities of all outlets is essential to provide the guest with quality service at all times.

The organisational chart of the key personnel of the food and beverage service department

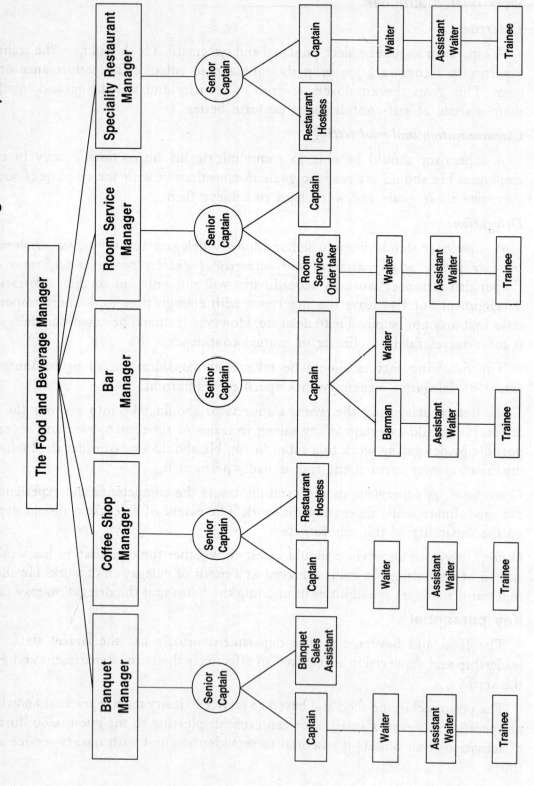

The food and beverage manager

The food and beverage manager is the head of the food and beverage service department, and is responsible for its administrative and operational work. It is said that a food and beverage manager is a Jack-of-all-trades, as the job covers a wide variety of duties.

Functions of the food and beverage manager

Budgeting

The food and beverage manager is responsible for preparing the budget for the department. He should ensure that each outlet in the department achieves the estimated profit margins.

Compiling new menus and wine lists

In consultation with the chef, and based on the availability of ingredients and prevailing trends, the food and beverage manager should update and if necessary, compile new menus. New and updated wine lists should also be introduced regularly.

Quality control

The food and beverage manager should ensure quality control in terms of efficiency in all service areas, by ascertaining that the staff are adequately trained in keeping with the standards of the unit.

Manpower development

The food and beverage manager is responsible for recruitment, promotions, transfers and dismissals in the department. He should hold regular meetings with section heads, to ensure that both routine as well as projected activities of the department go on as planned. He should also analyse the shortcomings in the activities and ensure improvements.

In essence, the food and beverage manager's job involves :

- Setting objectives and monitoring performance.
- Formulating, planning and overseeing control systems by monitoring costs, sales and profit margins.
- Constantly evaluating systems and keeping the top management informed.
- Ordering of stocks.
- Planning menus.
- Training, motivating and effectively controlling staff.
- Co-ordinating all aspects of food and beverage operations.

Assistant food and beverage manager

This position exists only in large organisations. The assistant food and beverage manager assists the food and beverage manager in running the department by being more involved in the actual day-to-day operations.

An assistant food and beverage manager's job includes :

- Assisting section heads during busy periods.
- Taking charge of an outlet, when an outlet manager is on leave.
- Setting duty schedules for all the outlet managers and monitoring their performance.
- Running the department independently in the absence of the food and beverage manager.

Restaurant manager

The restaurant manager is either the coffee shop manager, bar manager or the speciality restaurant manager. The restaurant manager reports directly to the food and beverage manager and has overall responsibility for the organisation and administration of a particular outlet or a section of the food and beverage service department.

The restaurant manager's job includes :

- Setting and monitoring the standards of service in the outlets.
- Administrative duties such as setting duty charts, granting leave, monitoring staff positions, recommending staff promotions and handling issues relating to discipline.
- Training the staff by conducting a daily briefing in the outlet.
- Playing a vital role in public relations, meeting guests in the outlets and attending to guest complaints, if any.
- Formulating the sales and expenditure budget for the outlet.
- Planning food festivals to increase the revenue of the outlet along with the chef and the food and beverage manager.

Room service manager

The room service manager reports directly to the food and beverage manager and is responsible for the room service outlet. The room service manager checks that the service rendered to the guests conforms to the standards set by the hotel. He also monitors all operational aspects of the outlet such as service, billing, duty charts, leave and absenteeism, in addition to attending to guest complaints regarding food and service.

The room service manager is also in charge of the sales and expenditure budget. Since room service is the outlet which is most liable to have problems, the room service manager should ensure coordination among the room service order taker, the captain and the waiter. It is necessary for the room service manager to be present in the outlet during peak hours to interact with other departments of the hotel and to take regular inventories of all the equipment used. In the event of the hotel offering valet service, the room service manager takes charge of that service as well.

Banquet manager

The banquet manager too is responsible for the functioning of his outlet, but as the banquet outlet is a major revenue earner in the food and beverage department, the work load is more intense and heavier.

From the time the bookings are done till the guest settles the bill, the banquet manager is in charge of all areas of banquet and conference operations. He supervises the work of the banquet sales assistants who do the banquet bookings and the captains and waiters who perform the service activities under his guidance. He is responsible for organising everything right down to the finest detail.

The banquet manager projects the budget of the banquets, and works in close coordination with the chef in setting menus. He is responsible for making an inventory of all the banquet equipment and maintaining a balance between revenue and expenditure.

Banquet managers may also be designated as *assistant managers* in the food and beverage service department.

Assistant banquet manager

Depending upon the size of the establishment and the number of banquet halls, there may also be an assistant banquet manager who maintains banquet records, takes bookings and monitors correspondence. In short, he ensures the smooth operation of all functions, by giving clear and precise instructions to the concerned staff. This job can also be done by a banquet sales executive or banquet sales assistant.

The assistant banquet manager is in charge of the actual performance of the functions held in the banquet department. He coordinates with the senior captain and is in charge of inventories, billing and briefing. He also deals with complaints from the guests and liaisons with various agencies for banquet requirements.

The assistant banquet manager should be aware of all that is happening in the banquet outlet, as he is responsible for the success of each banquet from the beginning to the end. In short, an assistant banquet manager performs both the functions of managing the office and monitoring banquet operations.

Banquet sales assistants

They are responsible for managing the banquet reservation system in the banquet office. They normally work in shifts and take bookings for all functions to be held in the hotel. They prepare the *Function Prospectus* (FP) or *Banquet Function Contract* (BFC) that contains all the details of the proposed function, according to the guest's needs. They coordinate closely with the banquet operational staff to ensure that the function is planned as specified in the booking form. They interact closely with the other departments of the hotel, on behalf of the operational team in the banquets. They report to the banquet manager.

Teamwork is the watchword in any food and beverage service department. A dedicated and committed team, with able leadership, under ideal working conditions, helps in fulfilling the establishment's ultimate goal of guest satisfaction.

Organisational hierarchy

To ably support the key personnel of the food and beverage service department in various operations, the staffing is further structured by a system of grades, and each grade carries a designation with a clearly identified responsibility and accountability to one's immediate superior. In this way delegation is structured down the line, where a member of staff at each level is responsible for the performance of his job which, to a certain extent is dependent on a subordinate's performance.

The following are the various designations with their job specifications in the food and beverage department.

Senior captain or Maître d'hôtel

The senior captain has overall responsibility for operations. He prepares the duty charts in consultation with the outlet manager. He oversees the *mise-en-place*, cleaning, setting of the outlet and staffing to ensure that the outlet is always ready for service.

The senior captain receives the guests and hands them over to the captain or station holder. He takes orders from guests if the captain is unable to do so. The senior captain should be an able organiser and also be prepared to take over the duties of any member of the staff as and when required.

Captain or Chef de Rang

This position exists in large restaurants, as well as in the food and beverage service department of all major hotels. The captain is basically a supervisor, and is in charge of a particular section. A restaurant may be divided into sections called *stations,* each consisting of 4 to 5 tables or 20 to 24 covers. A captain is responsible for the efficient performance of the staff in his station. A captain should possess a sound knowledge of food and beverage, and be able to discuss the menu with the guests. He should be able to take a guest's order and be an efficient salesperson. Specialised service such as guéridon work involves a certain degree of skill, and it is the captain who usually takes the responsibility to do this work.

Waiters or Commis de Rang

The waiters serve the food and beverage ordered by a guest and are part of a team under a station captain. They should be able to perform the duties of a captain to a certain extent and replace the captain if he is busy or not on duty. They should also be knowledgeable about all types of food and beverages, so that they can effectively take an order from a guest, execute the order and serve the correct dish with its appropriate garnish and accompaniment. They should be able to efficiently coordinate with the other staff in the outlet.

Trainee or Commis de barraseur

The trainees work closely with the waiters, fetching orders from the kitchen and the bar, and clearing the side station in a restaurant. They serve water and assist the waiter. They are mainly responsible for the *mise-en-place,* and stacking the side board with the necessary equipment for service.

Wine waiter or Sommelier

This position is not very common in India. However, wine waiters have an important role to play in reputed establishments. Their job is to take orders for the service of wine and alcoholic beverages and serve them during the meal. Hence they should be knowledgeable about wines that accompany a particular dish and the manner in which they should be served. They should also be aware of the licensing laws prevalent in the city and should be efficient salespersons.

Room service waiters or Chef d'etage

Room service waiters work in the room service outlet, serving both food and beverage to guests in their rooms. The order is placed by the guest on telephone, and is recorded on a *Kitchen Order Ticket* (K.O.T). It is then passed on to the duty captain. The duty captain in turn places the order in the kitchen or the bar, as the case may be. The room service waiter who has been assigned that order, sets the tray according to the food or beverage ordered, picks up the order when it is ready, and serves it to the guest along with the check, either for payment or signature. In the latter case it would be settled when the guest checks out. The service should be prompt and efficient as one lapse means a complaint about service and a dissatisfied guest.

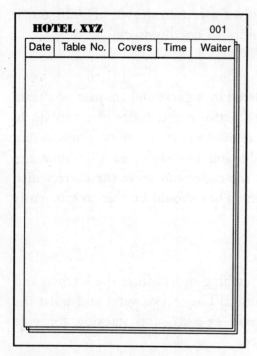

Fig. 4.1 *A kitchen order ticket (K.O.T)*

Fig. 4.2 *A food or beverage check of a room service outlet*

Room service order taker

A room service order taker records all orders of food and beverage from a resident guest over the telephone. She records the order on a Kitchen Order Ticket (K.O.T) and passes it to the captain. The captain in turn assigns it to a waiter who serves the order. The room service order taker is responsible for all communication between the guest and the staff of the room service outlet and hence should have good communication skills.

Hostess

It is quite common in India to utilise the services of a hostess to greet and seat guests. The hostess presents to the guests the menu card and hands them over to the station holder to continue service. She should be pleasant and well organised; be able to work under stress and interact smoothly with her colleagues.

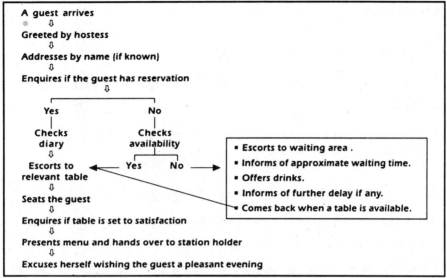

Fig. 4.3 *A flow chart showing how to seat a guest*

Barman

A barman works behind the bar counter dispensing beverage and making cocktails. He should have pleasant manners, good communication skills and a sound knowledge of all beverages and mixes. He should be fast and efficient.

Cashier

The main duty of a cashier is to make checks on the basis of the Kitchen Order Tickets (K.O.T). Most cash counters are computerised. Though cashiers are not a part of the food and beverage team, they work closely in association with the staff of the department. They report directly to the accountant.

All the staff working in the food and beverage department should have a thorough knowledge of the entire range of food and beverages served, with their correct accompaniments, garnishes, service temperature of each dish and beverage and the sequence in which they are to be served.

SUMMARY

1. A supervisor is a link in implementing the management's plans.
2. The key personnel of the food and beverage service department perform diverse tasks.
3. The food and beverage manager leads the food and beverage service department and delegates tasks to the other personnel who report to him.
4. The staff of the food and beverage service department work as a team in the performance of their duties to achieve total guest satisfaction.

Review Questions

Answer the following questions :

1. What is supervision and what role does a supervisor play in the performance of tasks?

2. List the qualities of an efficient supervisor.

3. Define the role of a food and beverage manager.

4. Explain the functions of a banquet manager.

5. Trace the hierarchy of the food and beverage service department and outline the job descriptions for each grade.

6. Describe how outlet managers contribute to the functioning of the food and beverage service department.

Projects

1. *Make a report on how you would fill the role of a supervisor in the food and beverage service department.*

2. *You are a food and beverage manager. Make a report on your plans for the forthcoming year.*

Glossary

Budgeting : An estimate of revenue or income and expenditure made by a company/unit/hotel.

Captain : A supervisor of service staff in the food and beverage service department.

Delegate : To entrust a task to another person.

Mise-en-place : A French term which means *to put in place.* This is a widely practised activity in all food and beverage service outlets.

Station : A section in a restaurant consisting of four to five tables or twenty to twenty-five covers.

Station holder : A waiter who serves a station consisting of four to five tables.

5

Attributes of Food and Beverage Service Personnel

■■■■■■■■■■■■■■■■■■■■■■■■■■■■■■■■

> **Objectives :** A study of this chapter will enable you to :
> ✧ *List the attributes of the food and beverage service personnel and their relevance to the hotel industry.*
> ✧ *Understand the responsibilities of the food and beverage service personnel.*
> ✧ *Discuss the significance of the quality of salesmanship among all food and beverage service personnel.*

Essential qualities of food and beverage service personnel

The quality of service staff in any establishment reflects the quality of the establishment. No matter how good the food and ambience are, poorly trained, untidy or rude staff can antagonize customers. On the other hand, if the staff are well-trained and efficient, they can, to a certain extent, make up for other shortcomings in the services provided.

Physical attributes

Personal hygiene and appearance

- All members of the staff should be well-groomed and clean at all times, as this gives them a sense of well-being and confidence to do their job efficiently.
- The hands of the waiting staff should be given special attention, as they are constantly under the scrutiny of guests. Nails should be trimmed, and kept clean. Playing with one's hair and face should be avoided.
- Chewing gum should be avoided in all public areas of the hotel.

- Minimum jewellery should be worn by the service staff. A wrist watch, a finger ring and plain earrings (for girls only) should be permitted.

- If an employee has a skin problem, a doctor should be consulted immediately.

- Uniform should be clean and well-pressed. Shoes should be properly polished and well-fitting.

Work related attributes

Good conduct : All service staff should be well-mannered and respectful to guests, and to senior members of the staff. They should be calm and pleasant, even in the most trying circumstances. They should be able to satisfactorily solve any problem that may arise. In case of difficulty, a senior and experienced member of the staff should be consulted. Tact, punctuality and honesty are admirable qualities among service personnel.

Salesmanship : The food and beverage service personnel are technical salespersons, hence they should have a thorough knowledge of the proper presentation and service of all the food and beverages served in the establishment. Waiters should be kept informed by their superiors of deletions or additions to the menu.

Good memory : A good memory helps to improve performance. It also helps the service personnel to attend to small but important details such as remembering a guest's name or his likes and dislikes regarding food and beverage.

Ability to assume responsibility : All service staff should be able to cope with the demands of the job and possess the ability to assume responsibility. They should be loyal to their employers, responsible to the guests and friendly towards their fellow workers. They should not consider any job as menial, and should be willing to perform all kinds of jobs efficiently. This will help the service staff to grow in their careers and at the same time enhance the image of the establishment in the eyes of the guests.

Maximise revenue : Cutting down on costs and maximising the revenue of the establishment should be of prime importance to all members of the staff, even to those in junior positions.

Observation : A keen sense of observation and an eye for detail will help a member of the staff to be more efficient at his job. An ability to correctly judge people, is definitely an advantage. A sense of anticipation in the service industry is an invaluable quality. The ability to anticipate what a guest or the management needs, even before it is asked for creates a very good impression.

Concentration and skill : Waiting at a table requires concentration and skill. Service staff should develop a sense of urgency in the performance of their duties. Good service may not be commented upon, but bad service is surely noticed and talked about. Service should be prompt without the show of haste.

In addition to these work related attributes, *knowledge of one or more languages* besides the regional language would be an asset to all service personnel. Familiarity with the city where one is working is important, as service staff may be called upon to answer queries or guide guests from time to time.

In short, service personnel should possess qualities such as *courtesy, cooperation, honesty, punctuality, tact, a good memory and a considerable knowledge of food and beverages.*

Some things that efficient service personnel should avoid

- *A surly greeting or not greeting a guest at all or ignoring a guest deliberately.*
- *Letting guests seat themselves, inspite of being present near the table and not otherwise engaged.*
- *Refusing to assist a guest or seating a guest at a dirty table.*
- *Serving from the wrong side, when it is possible to serve from the correct side.*
- *Not setting tables properly. Placing empty sugar bowls/cruet sets on the table.*
- *Forgetting to say 'Pardon me', or 'Excuse me, sir/madam'.*
- *Being too familiar with guests. This could lead to embarrassing situations.*
- *Gathering in groups in operational areas and talking loudly and showing signs of irritability with other members of the staff.*
- *Leaving fingerprints on crockery/glassware or making a noise by clattering the service equipment.*
- *Keeping the side station dirty or using torn or stained linen.*
- *Forgetting a dish that has been ordered, or serving wrong accompaniments.*
- *Overfilling water glasses or leaving them empty or leaving dirty ashtrays on an occupied table.*
- *Being inattentive to a guest's needs, for example, forgetting special instructions from the guest such as less chillies or no onions in the food.*
- *Using cold plates for hot food and hot plates for cold food.*
- *Touching food with one's hands.*
- *Not following the rules of quality waiting at table.*
- *Soliciting tips or questioning the amount of tips.*

Some useful phrases that may be used by service personnel

When seating a guest	: *Allow me, sir/madam.*
After seating a guest	: *Are you comfortable, sir/madam?*
To interrupt a guest at his meal to indicate that there is a call or a message	: *Sorry to intrude sir/madam; you have a call from ....*
(Do not disclose to the calling party that the guest is present until you check with the guest)	
While guiding a guest to a location	: *May I lead the way, sir/madam, or Please follow me, sir/madam.*
When opening a door for a guest	: *This way, sir/madam. After you, sir/madam.*
While serving breakfast in a guest's room	: *Present a newspaper, opened with the headlines facing the guest. Good Morning Mr./Mrs. ....*
	After placing the tray/trolley, draw the curtains in the room after inquiring from the guest. May I draw the curtains, sir/madam?
After drawing the curtains inform the guest about the weather	: *Fine morning, sir/madam. The sky is overcast, sir/madam. It's raining, sir/madam.*
(The state of the weather may influence the guest's programme for the day)	
When a guest cannot be attended to immediately	: *I will be with you in a few minutes, sir/madam.*
On recognizing a guest who has made a repeat visit to the restaurant or hotel	: *Good .... (time of the day) Mr/Mrs. .... (name of the guest) Nice to see you at the .... (name of the hotel or outlet). Welcome back.*
When offering a repeat drink	: *Would you care for a refill? May I top your glass up?*
While offering *seconds*, hold the food away from the guest's face and enquire	: *May I serve you some more........, (name of the dish) sir/madam? or Would you care for some more........, (name of the dish) sir/madam?*
To inform the host at a banquet party that the meal is ready to be served.	: *We are ready when you are, sir/madam.*
While circulating among guests in a cocktail party	: *I hope you are being looked after, sir/madam? Are you being served, sir/madam? May I fetch you a drink, sir/madam?*

While pouring water	:	*May I, sir/madam?*
If the guest does not want ordinary tap water, check by asking	:	*May I serve you some mineral water, sir/madam?*
While placing the ordered items in front of the guest	:	*Your ...., (name of the dish) sir/madam*
On enquiring about the meal	:	*Are you enjoying the food, sir/madam?*
While clearing	:	*I hope you have enjoyed your ...., (name of the dish) sir/madam*
On offering something complimentary to the guest	:	*With the compliments of .... (name of the manager) or With the compliments of the .... (name of the outlet)*
When a guest thanks for good service	:	*It's a pleasure to serve you, sir/madam. It's nice to have you with us, sir/madam. Please do visit again.*

Seven phrases to suit most of the occasions

Certainly, sir/madam.

Very well, sir/madam.

It's a pleasure, sir/madam.

I'll do that right away, sir/madam.

That should be no problem, sir/madam.

Right away, sir/madam.

May I be of assistance, sir/madam?

SUMMARY

1. All service personnel should be well-groomed, alert and professional.
2. All service personnel should have a thorough knowledge of all food and beverages, their proper presentation and service.
3. All service personnel should be courteous to the guests.

Review Questions

Answer the following questions :

1. List any four good habits of personal hygiene that should be followed by the service personnel.

2. Explain the statement *All food and beverage service personnel are technical salespersons.*

3. List any six things that efficient service personnel should avoid.

4. Describe how each of the work related attributes affects the performance of the service personnel.

5. For each of the following situations give examples of the appropriate phrases service personnel should use.
   i. While opening a door for the guest.
   ii. On recognizing a guest who has made a repeat visit to the hotel/restaurant.
   iii. When a guest cannot be attended to immediately.
   iv. When a guest thanks for good service.
   v. While placing the ordered items in front of the guest.

Projects

1. *Imagine you are a restaurant manager. Prepare a checklist highlighting the various physical attributes of the service personnel.*

2. *Develop an appraisal form for the work related attributes of the service personnel.*

Glossary

Briefing : The act of giving pertinent instructions, before the commencement of service.

Complimentary : Something given free of charge as a gesture of goodwill.

Food service personnel : Staff of a catering establishment involved in the exercise of providing service to guests.

Operational areas : All areas pertaining to activities conducted in the food and beverage department.

Seconds : A second helping of food at a meal or a second helping of the same dish.

Sense of anticipation : A sense of looking forward to.

Technical salesperson : A person who uses his knowledge of a product to sell it to customers.

Waiting at table : The skill of professional service of food and beverage.

6

Food and Beverage Service Skills

● ●

> **Objectives :** A study of this chapter will enable you to :
> ✧ *Understand the terms mise-en-scene, mise-en-place and cover.*
> ✧ *Handle crockery, cutlery and glassware properly.*
> ✧ *Categorise the duties of a waiter.*
> ✧ *Identify the various types of service practised in the catering industry.*
> ✧ *Describe the correct sequence of service and identify its importance.*

The service of food and beverage

The service of food and beverage needs professional expertise. The service should *follow a sequence* and *have a plan of action* based on the established practices of the professional catering industry. To ensure that the plan is followed, the service staff should perform certain tasks before, during and after service.

Duties of a waiter

Before the guests arrive :

The waiter should ensure that :

- The tables and linen are clean. Tablecloths are evenly spread on all sides.
- Chairs are dusted and properly arranged.
- The table set up is correct, the silver is polished and the china and glassware are spotlessly clean.
- Cruet sets, sugar bowls and flower vases are filled and placed correctly on the table.
- The floor/carpet is clean and dry.

- The restaurant and back area are in a state of readiness before the service session commences.
- The side station is fully equipped for service and the following should be checked regarding the side station :
  - *Condiments tray is cleaned and refilled.*
  - *Napkins are folded and kept handy for the particular session.*
  - *Salvers, extra linen, cutlery and service equipment necessary for the session are stacked in the side station.*
  - *Water jugs and ice buckets are filled and kept on each side station.*

When the guests arrive :

- Greet the guests warmly, by wishing them the time of the day.
- Escort the guests to the table and seat them promptly by pulling the chairs out to ease seating. If need be, the table should be moved so that very little inconvenience is caused to guests when they seat themselves.
- Ensure that children have high chairs and special attention is paid to the elderly.
- Remove extra covers, if any.
- Serve water and present the menu card, if the captain is busy.
- If the order has to be taken, offer suggestions to the guests in the choice of food and beverages and repeat the final order to avoid any error.

During the meal :

- Do not leave the station unattended, as nothing annoys a guest more than not being able to find a waiter, when something is needed.

- If the tablecloth has to be changed during service, the felt covered table top should not be exposed. Any articles on the table should be cleared to the side station and *not placed on chairs or on the next table.*

The soiled cloth should be brushed using a service cloth and a crumbing tray or plate.

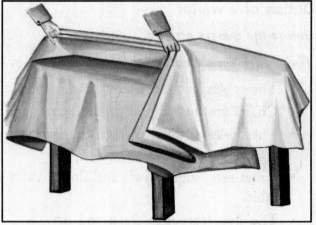

Fig. 6.1 *Changing a tablecloth during service*

- Do not neglect little things such as lighting a guest's cigarette, responding to a request and showing interest in the guest's needs.

- Ensure that service is fast, efficient and pleasant. Before serving dessert, clear and crumb the table.

- Examine the check thoroughly before presenting it and do so only if asked for.

When the guests leave :

- Pull out the chairs or the table to enable guests to move out comfortably.

- Warmly wish them and request them to visit again, saying — *Do visit again, sir/madam.*

- Clear the table immediately and reset for the next guest.

- Have the side station cleared and restacked for the next sitting.

Mise-en-scene

This French term means to *prepare the environment of the outlet* before service. It involves cleaning the service area, tables, chairs, side station, trolleys or any other service equipment. This operation generally precedes *mise-en-place.*

Mise-en-place

This French term means to *put in place.* It is widely used in the food and beverage service department in everyday hotel operations. Before service commences, the staff should ensure that the outlet is in total readiness to receive guests. This is an ongoing process and needs to be done in all outlets of the food and beverage service department.

Mise-en-place involves :

- Side stations should be stacked with sufficient covers for resetting the restaurant after the first sitting is over. Extra linen, crockery, cutlery, glassware and ashtrays should be kept handy so that they are readily available for use.

- Cruet sets should be cleaned and filled on a daily basis.

- Sauce bottles should be filled and the necks and tops of the bottles wiped clean.

- Butter, condiments and accompaniments for service should be kept ready for use when needed.

Basic rules for laying a table

- The table on which a tablecloth is to be spread, should be first covered with a *baize base cloth,* for the following reasons :

  - *To protect the diner's wrists and elbows from the table's sharp edges.*
  - *To keep the tablecloth firmly in place.*
  - *To protect the surface of the table and prevent the rattling of crockery and cutlery.*
  - *To absorb moisture in case liquid spills on the table.*

- Based on the size of the table, appropriate linen should be used. The central fold of the tablecloth should be in the middle of the table and all the four edges should just brush the seats of the chairs. Soiled or torn linen should not be used. Three types of tablecloths namely *cotton, linen* and *damask* are used, of these, damask is the best.

- If a bud vase is used as a central decorative piece, it should not be very large or tall as that obstructs the view of guests sitting opposite each other. Heavily scented flowers should be avoided, as they affect the flavour of the food.

- Each *cover* should be well-balanced. *A cover is the space required on a table for laying cutlery, crockery, glassware and linen for one person to partake of a meal.* Only the required cutlery, crockery and glassware should be placed on the table. On a normal dining table, the space required for one cover is 60 cm x 38 cm. The cover on the opposite side should be exactly similar, so as to give a well-balanced look.

- Cutlery should always be laid from the inside to the outside of the cover, since the order of sequence in which they are to be used is always from outside to inside.

Fig. 6.2 *Cover for a 'fixed or table d'hôte menu'*

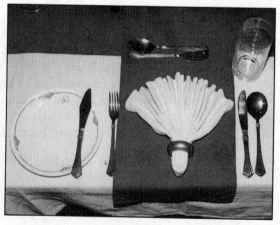

Fig. 6.3 *Cover for an 'a la carte menu'*

- Knives and soup spoons should be placed on the right-hand side of a cover, while forks should be placed on the left-hand side. Dessert spoons and forks should be placed on top of the cover. The side knife should be placed on a quarter plate and kept on the left side of the cover. The cutting edge of all knives should face to the left.

- Water tumbler should be kept to the right of the cover, at the tip of the large knife.

- Napkins should be placed in the centre of the cover, in between the cutlery. Normally during a dinner session, napkins are arranged in empty water tumblers.

- Cruet sets, a butter dish, an ashtray, meal accompaniments and a bud vase should be placed in between the covers at the centre of the table.

- Crockery and cutlery should be spotlessly clean and the glassware well polished. Chipped or cracked equipment should not be used. The hotel's monogram should be visible to the guest.

- All cutlery and crockery, should be placed about half an inch from the edge of the table so that they are not accidentally tipped over.

The correct handling of crockery, cutlery and glassware

- The basic rule is to avoid touching/handling any part of the crockery, cutlery or glassware which comes in direct contact with the food or the guest's mouth.

- Spoons, forks and knives should always be held by their handles and not by the bowls, prongs or blades.

- A waiter's cloth or a napkin should be used while laying or removing cutlery.

Fig. 6.4 *Carrying glassware on a salver*

Fig. 6.5 *Carrying stemmed glassware without a salver*

- Cutlery which has accidentally fallen down, should be replaced immediately.

- Cups should be carried by their handles and not by their rims.

- A clean waiter's cloth should be used to handle a hot plate or it should be held by the rim, so that a minimum of the plate's surface is touched.

- Glasses should be picked up by their base to avoid fingerprints on the polished surface.

- Glasses with stems should be carried on a salver, or upside down with the stems held between the fingers.

Rules for waiting at a table

- Check if the restaurant is clean and set according to the plan. Also check if the *mise-en-place* is completed.

- Study the menu of the day carefully, and find out from the kitchen, the dishes that are not available and the specials for the day.

- While taking orders, do not rest your hand on the corner of the table or on the back of the chair. Avoid leaning over the guest. Do not make misleading statements to guests regarding the quality of food, or the time it takes to prepare a dish.

- Wipe the rims of all plates and the bottoms of all dishes before carrying them to the table. Do not serve food or beverage in a plate or a glass that is not dry or clean.

- Announce the name of the dish you are about to serve. If a guest is reading a newspaper, or is in the middle of a conversation, do not interrupt rudely, but excuse yourself politely and ask for permission to serve the food. After service, stand at a respectful distance from the table.

- See that each guest is served with water throughout the meal and try to anticipate the requirements of the guest.

- Hot food should be served in hot plates and cold food should be served in cold plates. Avoid filling glasses and cups to the brim. Do not put a spoon in a guest's plate or cup, allow the guest to do it himself.

- Do not use a dirty napkin or waiter's cloth. If any piece of equipment falls on the floor, replace it from the side station immediately.

- The menu card should be placed on the side station after use. It should not be left lying on the table or tucked into the waiter's pocket.

- Service should be prompt, efficient and unobtrusive.

Types of table service

The food and beverage service industry is vast and complex, catering to an amazing mix of clientele, ranging from the modest to the affluent. Accordingly, there are various types of service that are classified based on the *category of guests to be served* and *the sequence of operations* to be followed.

The following are some of the popular types of service offered to the guests.

Silver service

This is a form of table service, where the waiter serves the food to the guest at the table. The food is picked up from the kitchen, taken to the hot plate on the side station on platters and presented to the guest. Before service the waiter should ensure that the food is served onto the guest's plate in a stylish and efficient manner, recreating the arrangement on the platter. This type of service demands skill on the part of the waiter in handling a service spoon and fork and an organised way of functioning, so that the courses follow one another at proper intervals.

Fig. 6.6 *Use of service spoon and fork for 'silver service'*

Plated-cum-silver service

This service is offered when the menu is a *table d'hôte* menu. For this form of service, the main course is plated in the kitchen, while the accompaniments of vegetables, potatoes and sauces are served from *entrée* dishes, using a service spoon and fork.

American or pre-plated service

This form of service is normally found in restaurants which have a large guest turnover. The food is pre-plated in the kitchen and served to the guest. The waiter ensures that the necessary accompaniments are already placed on the table, and the correct cover has been laid before service.

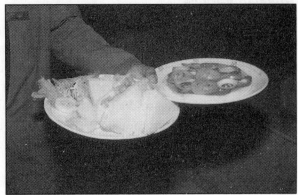

Fig. 6.7 *American or pre-plated service*

English service

In this form of service, the main dish is meat. It is carved by the host and served by the waiter to the guests. Vegetables and potatoes are placed at the centre of the table for guests to help themselves while sauces are served by the waiter.

French service

This service involves bringing food from the kitchen in *entrèe* dishes or oval flats and placing them on the table. The plates are kept next to the dishes and the guests serve themselves.

Guéridon service

The word *guéridon* means *a mobile table or trolley which is brought close to the guests' table.* This type of service involves the use of a guéridon trolley. It requires the waiter to be a showman as well as a good cook. He should be skilled and possess the ability to *carve* a joint of meat, *fillet* a fish, *prepare* a grapefruit cocktail, *flambé* a variety of dishes and *prepare* several types of coffee such as Irish coffee and snake coffee, using the guéridon trolley which is placed in front of the guest's table. In other words, he should be able to prepare a full meal in front of the guest or give finishing touches to the food that is partially cooked in the kitchen.

Fig. 6.8 *Guéridon service*

Russian service

This is a fairly elaborate service involving the use of a **guéridon** trolley in the restaurant. The food is taken directly on the guéridon trolley which is placed near the guests' table. The waiter pre-portions the food and serves it onto the guest's plate, and then places the plate in front of the guest. Presentation is an important aspect of this service and at times, whole joints of meat, game, fish or poultry are presented to the guest before being carved by the waiter and served.

Buffet service

A *buffet* is a table or a counter set with all the cooked food stylishly displayed. There are two forms of buffet service — a *sit-down* buffet and a *fork* buffet.

Sit-down buffet

The guest picks up the food from the buffet counter, and sits down at a table which is pre-set with covers as in a restaurant.

Fork buffet

This type of service does not provide any seating arrangements. The guest uses a fork and eats standing, holding his plate.

Counter service

This kind of service is offered in cafés and is very popular in western countries. Here the guest sits at the serving counter and the food is served and consumed at the counter itself. Sometimes covers are arranged at the counter.

Cafeteria service

This type of service is very common in schools and institutions. The guest picks up a tray and selects the food from the display counters. At the end of the service counter, a cashier totals up the cost of the meal by checking the food on the tray. The guest pays for the meal before going to the dining section.

Take-aways

In this kind of service, the food is ordered to be packed and taken away. In the USA there are *drive-in take-aways,* where orders are placed, collected and paid for at successive points, thus saving time and increasing the speed of service.

Food courts

This service is growing in popularity and it probably won't be long before food courts appear in India. This service involves the preparation of food in different kitchens, each representing a different cuisine. The food is picked up from each individual section and eaten at a common dining area.

Room service

This relates to service of food to guests in their rooms, by waiters who pick up the food from the kitchen. The order is received from the guest generally over the telephone by the room service department and then served in the room.

Bar service

This is similar to counter service and is predominantly used in cocktail bars where guests sit on bar stools at the counter and a variety of beverages are served from behind the bar counter.

Services available in a food and beverage service department

Bed tea or coffee

This service is offered through room service, and is normally accompanied with cookies.

Breakfast

This service may be offered in any food and beverage outlet. It includes the service of Continental, American, English and Indian breakfasts. This may be from an *a la carte* menu, a *table d'hôte* menu or a *buffet breakfast* menu.

Brunch

This form of service is growing in popularity, especially on Sundays and holidays. It includes service of breakfast and some selected light lunch items normally after 11 am, that is, between breakfast and lunch time.

Lunch

Service of lunch may take place in any food and beverage outlet, and could include food from a variety of cuisines. It is served in the afternoon between 12 noon and 3 pm.

Afternoon tea

This is service of tea or coffee with some light snacks such as sandwiches or cookies. It is normally served around 4 pm.

High tea

This is served usually around 6 pm, and involves the service of some substantial snack along with tea or coffee.

Dinner

Like lunch, dinner is served in most food and beverage service outlets and consists of food from several styles of cooking. Service takes place in the evening between 7:30 pm and midnight.

Supper

This is a very difficult meal to explain in the context of meal timings in India. Supper is popular in Europe, and is normally an early dinner very often associated with the theatre, as diners have a light supper, attend the theatre and may later have a heavy dinner.

Midnight snack

Coffee shops and room service outlets provide some selected snacks that are available throughout the night.

SUMMARY

1. The service of food and beverages should follow a sequence and a plan of action based on the established practices of the professional catering industry.

2. The duties of a waiter include tasks to be done before the guests arrive, when the guests arrive, during the meals and when the guests leave.

3. *Mise-en-scene* means *to prepare the environment of the outlet before service. Mise-en-place* is a French term which means *to put in place* that is, to keep the outlet in total readiness to receive guests. These are widely practised activities in all food and beverage service outlets.

4. Several basic rules should be followed for laying a table to ensure that the highest standards of service are offered to guests.

5. The practice of good service techniques begins with the correct handling of cutlery, crockery and glassware as well as following the rules for waiting at table.

6. Each type of service offered is classified by the category of clientele to be served and the sequence of operations.

Review Questions

Answer the following questions :

1. Describe the variety of services available based on the established practices of the professional catering industry.

2. Briefly outline the sequence of services to be followed when a guest arrives at a restaurant in a five star hotel.

3. Define the· terms *mise-en-scene* and *mise-en-place.*

4. List the basic rules for laying a table in a restaurant.

5. How should crockery, cutlery and glassware be handled in an outlet?

6. Highlight the basic rules for waiting at a table.

7. Name the different types of service of food and beverage one may find in the course of a day in a hotel.

Projects

1. *Make a report of how you would follow the service sequence based on the established practices of the professional catering industry.*

2. *Visit any three food service operations and record your observations of the type of service being followed in the food and beverage department.*

Glossary

Accompaniments : Served along with the food or beverage to enhance its taste and flavour.

Baize base cloth : Soft felt cloth usually green in colour used on most dining tables in restaurants and banquets.

Buffet : A meal consisting of several dishes, attractively displayed on a counter or table, from which guests can serve themselves.

Carve : To cut meat or poultry (at times done at the table) into slices.

Condiments tray : A tray used to hold spices that are put directly on the food by the guest.

Cover : The space required on a table for laying cutlery, crockery, glassware and linen for one person to partake of a meal.

Crumb a table : Brushing the crumbs dropped on the tablecloth after a meal, using a waiter's cloth.

Cuisine : A style or a method of cooking. It also means *kitchen* in French.

Entrée dish : An oval dish that is used to serve food to a guest.

Fillet a fish : A cut of fish from which the bones are removed.

Mise-en-scene : A French word that means *to prepare the environment.*

Mise-en-place : A French term meaning *to put in place and be ready for service.*

Oval flat : An oval-shaped flat service platter that comes in several sizes.

Pre-plated : Food put on the plate in the kitchen and served; the guest eats out of the same plate.

7

Service Equipment

Objectives : A study of this chapter would enable you to :

✧ *Name the various types of service equipment used in the food and beverage service department.*

✧ *Mention the criteria for selecting service equipment.*

✧ *Describe the standard sizes, uses and upkeep of the crockery, cutlery, glassware and holloware used in different outlets in the food and beverage service department.*

The service equipment used in hotels/restaurants plays an important role in attracting customers. Attractive serviceware, colourful and clean dishes, plates and glassware add to the decor of a restaurant. The choice of service equipment usually reflects the standard and style of a restaurant. However, several factors have to be considered while selecting the equipment. A hotel/restaurant should be well-stocked with appropriate equipment to provide quality service. For multipurpose use and to cut down costs, most hotels/restaurants standardise equipment in terms of size and colour.

Criteria for selecting service equipment

- Types of service offered and the category of guests entertained.
- The size of the outlet.
- The layout of the food and beverage service area.
- Durability of the equipment, cost and ease of maintenance.
- Availability of stock, facility of its storage and flexibility of use.
- Price factor, availability of funds and standardisation.
- Design, shape and colour, and delivery time of equipment.

Restaurant furniture

The atmosphere of a restaurant is largely affected by the kind of furniture used. The furniture should be utilitarian but elegant to look at.

Tables

The size and shape of tables depends entirely on the availability of space and the kind of service envisaged. Normally three types of tables are used. They are *round, rectangular* and *square*.

The height of the table irrespective of the shape should be 75 cm from the floor level. The diameter of a round table to seat four people should be approximately 92 cm. The size of a square table to seat two people should be 76 cm sq and 92 cm sq to seat four people. The size of a rectangular table to seat four people should be 137 cm x 76 cm.

Chairs

The dimension of chairs should be relative to table dimensions. The average height of the chair should be 92 cm. The seat should be 46 cm from the floor and 23 cm from the top of the table. This would enable guests to sit and eat comfortably, without their legs touching the underside of the table.

Side station

This is a very important piece of furniture in a restaurant. It is used by the service staff for keeping all the service equipment at one place. It is also used as a landing table for the dishes picked up from the kitchen *enroute* to the table and the dirty dishes from the guest's table to the wash-up area. For the convenience of the service staff, the side station should be strategically located in a restaurant. The side station should be kept clean and presentable as it can be seen by the guests.

The following service equipment can be stored in a side station.

- Salvers
- Coffee pots
- Finger bowls
- Soup ladles
- Cigar cutters
- Candle holders
- Toothpick stand

- Creamers
- Teapots
- Cruet sets
- Butter dishes
- Bread baskets
- Wine cradle
- Straw stand

- Wine chiller and stand
- Ice buckets and tongs
- Sugar bowls and tongs
- Bottle and wine openers
- Bud vases
- Tea strainers and drip bowls
- Pot holders

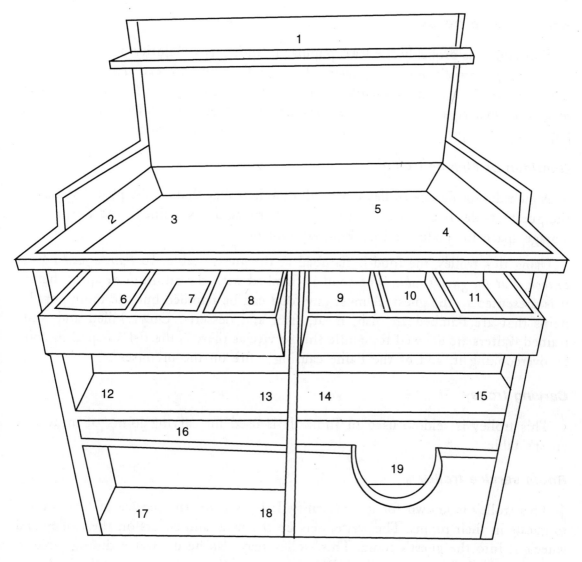

1. Sauce bottles	6. Service spoons and forks	10. Soup spoons	15. Ashtrays
2. Menu cards	7. All purpose spoons	11. Teaspoons	16. Salvers
3. K.O.T books	8. All purpose forks	12. Cups and saucers	17. Bread baskets
4. Water jugs	9. All purpose knives	13. Quarter plates	18. Fresh linen
5. Ice buckets		14. Glassware	19. Dirty linen

Fig. 7.1 *A side station*

Trolleys

The various trolleys used in the food and beverage service outlets are :

- Hors d'oeuvre trolley
- Guéridon or Flambé trolley
- Carving trolley
- Room service trolley
- Dessert trolley

Hors d'oeuvre trolley

This trolley is probably the least popular in India, as a majority of guests are not too keen on *hors d'oeuvre* as a starter. They prefer soups instead. An *hors d'oeuvre is the first course of a menu usually consisting of a selection of small items of egg, fish, meat, fruit and vegetables in pungent dressings.* However, this trolley can be used to popularise the special dishes that are introduced from time to time.

Guéridon or Flambé trolley

A guéridon or flambé trolley is a small mobile trolley that can be placed alongside the guest's table. It consists of one or two burners, a gas cylinder and a work and storage space for plates and cooking equipment.

Using this trolley, the food is flambéd at the guest's table. To *flambé food* means *to cook it at the guest's table.* The food is flambéd with the addition of spirit, before it is presented to the guest. Almost any food can be flambéd but the more popular items that are flambéd are fish, meat, fruit and desserts. Only skilled and well-trained waiters are allowed to handle this service as there is the risk of spoiling food by overcooking it, and of the flame causing a fire on the premises.

Carving trolley

This trolley is seldom used in India. It is used for carving joints of meat at a guest's table.

Room service trolley

This trolley is known for its versatility. It is used for the service of large orders to guests in their rooms. The waiter sets up the meal and covers on the trolley and wheels it into the guest's room. This trolley may also be used as a dining table in the privacy of the guest's room. Beneath the trolley top, provision is made for mounting a hot case to keep the food warm.

Dessert trolley

This trolley serves as a visual aid to selling desserts. Guests are more likely to order a dessert if they can see what is available, particularly if it is well presented. Some dessert trolleys are refrigerated. Gateaux, pastries, jellies, tarts, pies, flans and soufflés can be served from a dessert trolley.

This trolley has several shelves and the bottom shelf is reserved for plates, cutlery, linen and other service equipment. A glass or transparent trolley top makes it easy for guests to select a dessert of their choice.

Bar equipment

A bar should be well-stocked with essential equipment to carry out efficient service of alcoholic and non-alcoholic beverages.

Some essential bar equipment include:

- Assorted glassware
- Cutting boards and knives
- Ice buckets and tongs
- Water jugs
- Bottle coolers

- Service salvers
- Optics/peg measures
- Ice machine
- Decanters
- Coasters

- Cocktail shakers
- Lemon squeezers
- Bottle/wine openers
- Refrigerators
- Swizzle sticks

Linen

Tablecloths, napkins and slip cloths are usually described as linen. A good hotel/restaurant will normally use damask for all food and beverage service linen.

Tablecloths

Tablecloths should be large enough to cover the top as well as a portion of the legs of a table without interfering with the guest's comfort while he is seated at the table.

The size of the tablecloth varies according to the size of the table it is required to cover.

Types of tables	Size of tables	Size of tablecloths
Square table	76 cm sq 92 cm sq	137 x 137 cm 183 x 183 cm
Rectangular table	136 x 76 cm	183 x 137 cm
Round table	92 cm diameter	184 cm diameter

For a buffet table, the minimum size of the tablecloth required is 2 m x 4 m.

Slip cloths or naperones

These are designed to be laid over the tablecloth to protect it from spillage and give it a longer life. Using a slip cloth, reduces the number of tablecloths used and thus reduces the cost of laundry. Slip cloths may measure 1 metre square approximately.

Napkins or serviettes

Napkins may be of the same colour as tablecloths, or in a colour that blends with the decor of the restaurant. Napkins should be **spotlessly clean** and **well-pressed**. The ideal size for a napkin is between 46 to 50 cm sq.

Napkin folding

Crisp, freshly laundered napkins are an essential feature of a well-set table. They can be pressed in large plain squares and laid at each cover with the minimum of fuss or folded in a variety of ways to *complement the food*, the *set up of the table* and the *occasion*.

Tips for successful folding

Well-starched plain napkins measuring 46 to 50 cm sq would be ideal for complicated folding techniques. The fabric should be cut square and straight on the weave so that the napkins do not pull out of shape easily. They should be washed, starched and ironed when damp. While ironing, the napkins should be pulled back gently into shape to ensure that they are perfectly square again.

While folding napkins into complicated shapes, each fold should be pressed separately. Soft folds should not be pressed.

Some popular napkin folds are the **cocked hat,** the **fan,** the **crown,** the **candle,** the **tent** and the **book fold.**

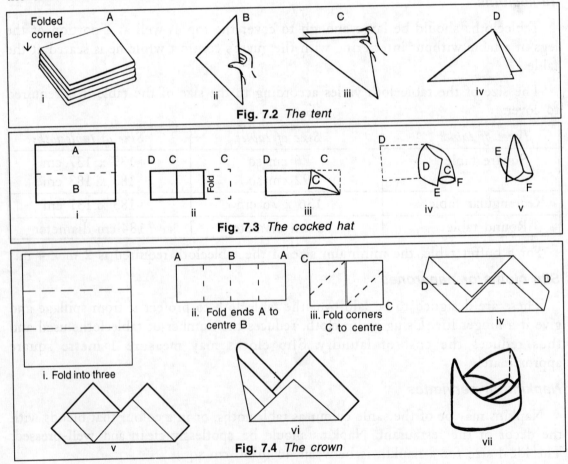

Fig. 7.2 *The tent*

Fig. 7.3 *The cocked hat*

ii. Fold ends A to centre B

iii. Fold corners C to centre

i. Fold into three

Fig. 7.4 *The crown*

Crockery or china

Crockery or chinaware is made of silica, soda ash and china clay and dry glazed to give it a fine finish. Chinaware is available in different designs and colours and is sometimes coated with patterns on top of the glazed ware. Chinaware is more resistant to heat than glassware. Petrified chinaware is stronger and chip resistant. Many large hotels and restaurants have their china custom-made with their own design and monogram printed on it.

Care of crockery

- All china should be handled with care as it is fragile and can break easily.
- It should be properly stacked.
- Crockery should be stored in a dust-free environment.
- Crockery should be rinsed and dried after washing so that no residual washing powder is left.
- Cracked or chipped crockery should not be used.

Chinaware with approximate sizes and capacities are given below:

Plates — Diameter	
Fish plate	20 cm
Full plate or dinner plate	25 cm
Soup plate (deep)	20 cm
Dessert plate or half plate	18 cm
Oval flat	30 cm in length

Capacity :	
Teacup	150 or 175 ml
Demitasse	160 ml
Soup bowl	300 ml

Silverware

Items made of electroplated nickel silver — e.p.n.s or stainless steel are also used in restaurants. Some of them are :

- Milk creamers
- Egg cups
- Condiment trays
- Sugar bowls
- Cruet sets
- Chinese service bowls
- Butter dishes
- Ashtrays
- Coffee pots and teapots

Glassware

Silver and soda ash are used for making glassware. Lead is added to make the glass crystal clear.

Glassware also contribute to the appearance of the table. Most hotels/restaurants use plain clear glassware although some high class restaurants use cut glassware.

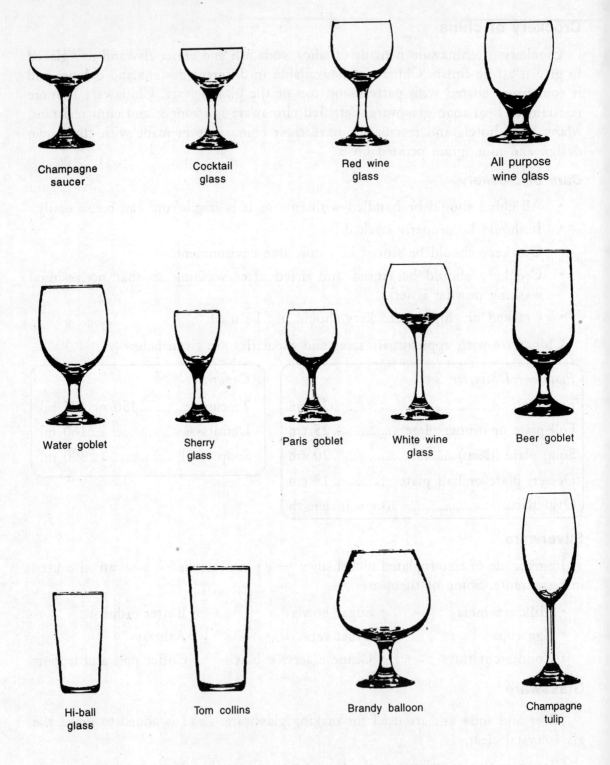

Fig 7.5 *Types of glassware*

Care of glassware

- While purchasing glassware, one should check that the glasses are transparent and free from air bubbles and pit holes.

- Glasses should be carefully washed in warm water and rinsed in clean hot water. They should be wiped dry using a linen cloth.

- Glassware should be kept inverted and neatly arranged in a row, either with a paper underliner or on a tray to avoid dust. Special plastic glass racks can also be used to stack glasses. These racks allow fresh air to circulate even when the glasses are overturned. They also facilitate smoother operations, especially in banquets.

- In a restaurant, glasses should not be carried on a plain salver, but with a tray mat to avoid slipping.

- Glasses should be vigorously polished and checked against light for smudges or fingerprints before use.

- Chipped or cracked glasses should not be used.

Cutlery

Different types of cutlery are used in hotels and restaurants.

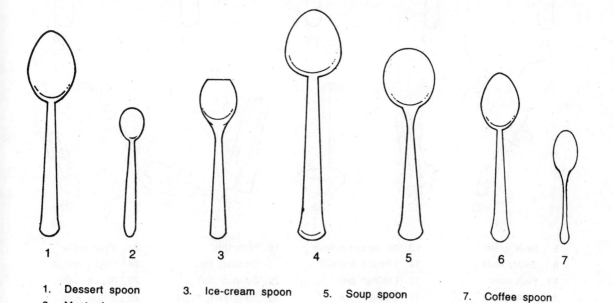

1. Dessert spoon
2. Mustard spoon
3. Ice-cream spoon
4. Service spoon
5. Soup spoon
6. Teaspoon
7. Coffee spoon

Fig 7.6A *Types of cutlery*

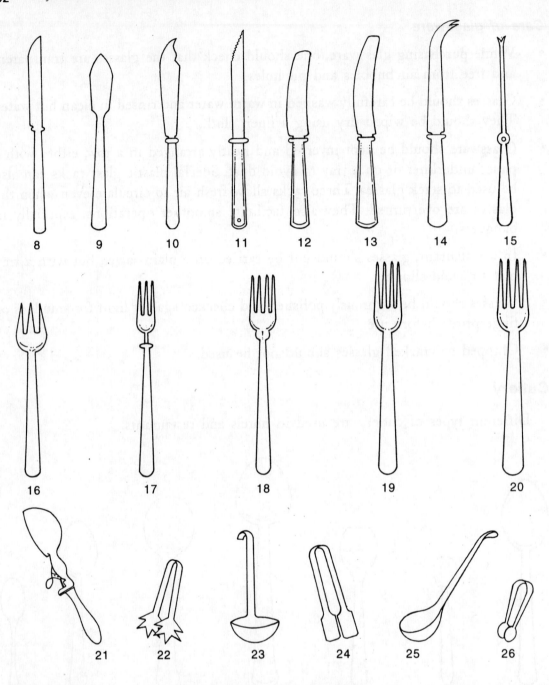

8. Fruit knife
9. Butter knife
10. Fish knife
11. Steak knife
12. Side knife

13. All purpose knife
14. Cheese knife
15. Lobster pick
16. Oyster fork
17. Fruit fork

18. Fish fork
19. Dessert fork
20. Service fork
21. Ice-cream scoop
22. Ice tongs

23. Soup ladle
24. Pastry tongs
25. Sauce ladle
26. Sugar tongs

Fig. 7.6B *Types of cutlery*

Holloware

This includes items made from silver or stainless steel. Some of the holloware used in hotels/restaurants are :

- Soup tureens
- Oval flats
- Prawn cocktail dishes

- Ice-cream bowls
- Entrèe dishes
- Chafing dishes

- Trays and platters
- Water jugs

The equipment used in a restaurant is an asset of the establishment and costs a considerable amount of money. Great care should be taken while handling it, and a strict control should be maintained on its *use, breakage and pilferage. Regular inventories* should be taken to keep a check on the costs and to identify the right time to make a purchase indent to replace equipment that is in short supply. *Stockpiling* of equipment that is not needed, should be avoided.

SUMMARY

1. The service equipment that is used in the food and beverage service industry is classified into crockery, cutlery, glassware and holloware.

2. Restaurant furniture and linen used in most service outlets are generally standardised in size and colour to cut down on costs.

3. Several types of trolleys are used in the food and beverage service department.

4. Crockery and glassware have different capacities and measurements depending upon their specific use during service.

5. Service equipment is considered to be an asset of an establishment, so it should be handled carefully.

Review Questions

Answer the following questions :

1. Describe the various types of service equipment used in the food and beverage service department.

2. List the main criteria for selecting service equipment.

3. Explain how you would set up a side station. List the equipment that can be stocked in it.

4. What care would you take in the use and storage of service equipment?

5. Explain the purpose of napkin folding.

Projects

1. *You are required to set up a 48-cover restaurant. List and justify the quantity and category of service equipment you would need.*

2. *Make a table to show the different sizes of furniture and linen you would need for your restaurant.*

Glossary

Chafing dish : A food warmer used during buffet service.

Coaster : A small mat put under a bottle or glass to avoid wet rings on the surface of the table.

Cutlery : Equipment used for eating and service, made from stainless steel or electroplated nickel silver — e.p.n.s.

Flambé : To pour alcohol over food and set it alight, to enhance visual delight during service.

Holloware : Equipment used for service of food. May be made from stainless steel or e.p.n.s.

Hot case : A metal case that keeps food hot. It is used with a room service trolley.

Inventory : Taking stock of equipment.

Monkey bowl : A small multipurpose bowl used for serving accompaniments.

Optics : A beverage control device used for measuring pegs of spirits before service.

Serviette or napkin : A square piece of cloth used to protect one's clothes and to wipe the mouth during a meal.

Station : A set of four or five tables in a restaurant.

Swizzle stick : A plastic or glass stirrer placed in cocktails to stir them.

8

Fundamentals of Menus

∎∎∎∎∎∎∎∎∎∎∎∎∎∎∎∎∎∎∎∎∎∎∎∎∎∎

> **Objectives :** A study of this chapter would enable you to :
>
> ❖ *Define the term menu, list the types of menus and how they are used in the catering industry.*
> ❖ *Explain the objectives of planning a menu.*
> ❖ *Discuss what is meant by compiling a menu and what are its main objectives.*
> ❖ *List and discuss the different courses in a French classical menu.*

What is a menu?

A menu is a list of food and beverage that can be served to a guest at a price. It helps guests to select what they would like to eat and/or drink. It is a document that controls and directs an outlet's operations and is considered the prime selling instrument.

The menu — *origin*

The word *menu* dates back to 1718, but the custom of making such a list is much older. In earlier times, the *escriteau* or *menu* (bill of fare) of ceremonial meals was displayed on the wall to enable the kitchen staff to follow the order in which the dishes were to be served. It is said that in olden times, menus were like a large dictionary with sections covering a variety of dishes. During the reign of Louis XIV, the variety and number of dishes served was unbelievable and guests tasted only a few of the dishes served. The *menu* or *bill of fare* was very long and it was placed at the end of the table to inform guests of what was being served. As time went by, the menu became smaller, and the number of dishes were divided into sections. In the early 19th century, guests in Parisian restaurants were given a small, handy reproduction of the menu displayed at the entrance.

> ### For interest
> *It is said that in the year 1541, Duke Henry of Brunswick used to refer to a long slip of paper, which listed the names of the numerous dishes to be served by his chef. By checking the contents of the list, he knew what was to follow and thus reserved his appetite accordingly.*

Functions of a menu

The menu in modern establishments reflects a concern for the health and well-being of the guests. The menu planners ensure a **healthy** and **balanced diet** for their guests without neglecting the pleasures of enjoying good food. The menu as we know it today, serves several purposes.

- A menu informs guests as to what dishes are available and the price charged for a particular dish.

- It enables guests to select dishes of their choice which they can afford.

- It guides the chef in the matter of his requirements in terms of staff, equipment and materials, to efficiently prepare the items included in the menu.

- It enables the service staff to prepare their *mise-en-place*, take the correct order, pick up and serve the correct dishes from the kitchen according to what has been ordered, and to present the correct check to the guest.

- It helps the management to work out the cost of the food and analyse the utility of a particular menu.

- It helps the cashier to price each item ordered by the guest and to prepare a sales summary, which is the sales history of the outlet.

- It enables the caterer to predict trends and to plan the future course of action for the outlet.

The menu and the caterer

The compilation of a menu is the most important part of a caterer's work. It is regarded as an art, acquired only through experience and study. The menu is a link between the guest and the establishment, hence it should be carefully planned by the establishment's professionals namely the *executive chef*, the *food and beverage manager* and the *food and beverage controller*.

Types of menus

There are two types of menus. (i) *Table d'hôte*   (ii) *A la carte*

Table d'hôte or a fixed menu

Table d'hôte refers to a *menu of limited choice*. It usually includes three or five courses available at a fixed price. It is also referred to as a *fixed menu*. This term is known to caterers by its abbreviation *TDH menu*. It means *from the table of the host*. In the past, it used to be offered by innkeepers to their guests at inns. When these dining establishments realised that offering a limited choice in the menu was not what discerning guests wanted, they started offering an *a la carte* menu for guests to select the type of food they wanted to eat.

Fixed menus or *table d'hôte* menus are still used in various forms such as *buffet menus, conference packages* and on *special occasions*. A *table d'hôte* menu comprises a *complete meal* at *a predetermined price*. It is sometimes printed on a menu card or as in the case of banquets, it is agreed upon by the host of the party. A banquet style of fixed menu has more elaborate choices ranging from the soup to the dessert.

As most of the banquet food served in India is normally Indian food, a printed format offering a choice of vegetarian and non-vegetarian dishes is prepared, from which the guests make their choice. Western style fixed menus normally provide the choice of a starter or soup, a main course, and finally a dessert. In each course there could be a choice of dishes to suit the tastes of individual guests.

Table d'hôte menus should be well planned and balanced. As the guest is not given a chance to plan his own meal, the meal should be interesting, without any similarity in the colour and taste of the courses, as well as being palatable and well presented. If the main course is heavy, then the first course should be lighter, and act as an appetite stimulant for the courses to follow. Dishes that are heavy and hard to digest should be avoided. The colour, varieties of ingredients used, and the garnishes should, if possible, be different in each course.

Menu

Seafood Cocktail
or
Mulligatawny Soup
or
Waldorf Salade
****

Fish Veronique
or
Chicken in Chasseur Sauce
or
Corn and Spinach Au Gratin
Served with fresh seasonal
vegetables and potatoes
****

Profit Rolls with Chocolate
Sauce
or
Lemon Soufflé
or
Orange Custard with Melba
Sauce
****

Filter Coffee or Tea
****

3 course meal Rs. 225/-[+]
[+]Inclusive of tax

Fig. 8.1 *An example of a 'table d'hôte menu'*

Fixed menus are prevalent in transport catering also. Air, rail and sea passengers have a variety of fixed or *table d'hôte* menus, with virtually no choice offered to the passenger (except the first class air passengers). Cruise liners may have elaborate fixed menus with multiple choices built into each course.

A la carte menu

An *a la carte* menu, is a *multiple choice menu*, with each dish priced separately. *A la carte* means *from the card*. If a guest wishes to place an order, an *a la carte* is offered, from which one can choose the items one wants to eat.

In an *a la carte* menu all items are cooked to order including the sauces that are made with wine, cream or mustard. Depending on the dish chosen by the guest, the cooking time will vary. It is necessary to inform guests about the time the preparation might take. An extensive *a la carte* menu is impressive but involves a huge amount of *mise-en-place*.

Nouvelle cuisine

This literally means *new style* of cooking. This concept was introduced in 1972 by two food critics, H. Gault and C. Millau, with the aim of encouraging a simpler and more natural presentation of food.

Menu

CONTINENTAL

Fresh Seasonal Juice .... Rs. 60.00
  Orange   Pineapple
  Tomato   Sweetlime

Fresh Seasonal Fruit .... Rs. 50.00
  Papaya   Pineapple
  Mango   Banana

Cereals .... Rs. 50.00
  Cornflakes
  Oatmeal with hot/cold milk

Eggs to order .... Rs. 65.00
  Fried   Scrambled
  Poached   Boiled

Served with Ham .... Rs. 80.00
  Bacon or Sausage

Omlettes .... Rs. 65.00
  Plain   Masala
  Ham & Cheese   Spanish

Oven Fresh Rolls Rs.40.00
  Croissant   Danish
  Muffin   Brioche
  Toast White/Brown

INDIAN

  Plain/Masala Dosa .... Rs. 50.00

  Idli/Vada .... Rs. 50.00
  Paneer/Aloo Parantha .... Rs. 65.00

Hot Beverage
  Tea/Coffee with milk/black ... Rs. 30.00
  Hot Chocolate .... Rs. 45.00
  Bournvita .... Rs. 45.00

Fig. 8.2 *An example of an 'a la carte menu'*

Advocates of nouvelle cuisine reject the rich, complicated and indigestible traditional food, that is no longer suitable for a generation conscious of the health hazards of overeating, especially of foods that are rich in fat.

The guiding principles of this cuisine are :

• the use of absolutely fresh ingredients
• the simplicity in the cooking method.

It also encourages the use of light sauces, based on meat extracts, stocks and herbs, and avoids the use of flour as a thickening agent. Vegetables are prepared in such a way that the natural flavours, colours and nutrients are retained. Rapid cooking without fat is done to retain the texture and nutritional value of the ingredients. The dishes are often served pre-plated and referred to as *art on the plate*.

Menu cards

A menu card is a document that is used as a **selling tool**. It helps in creating an image in the minds of guests about the class of the establishment. Hence care should be taken in the compilation of the menu, its presentation and format. Menu cards should be spotlessly clean, attractive and in pleasing colours. They should be available in sufficient numbers as they are to be presented not only to the host, but also to each guest.

The contents of the menu card indicate the dishes available in the outlet, and by proper menu management systems, one can generate the highest possible revenue for the establishment. The dishes listed on a menu card, should be described in simple and clear language. The prices should be indicated clearly. Items that are not available to the guest most of the time because of last minute changes due to equipment failure, non-delivery of raw materials or natural calamities should be deleted from the menu card. More popular dishes that would be available most of the time should be added to the list.

Planning a menu

Planning a menu is a complex managerial task. Costs, profit margins and gastronomic criteria have to be taken into account while planning a menu. Menus should be compiled to meet the requirements of various types of meals. If the menu fails to meet the market requirements, it could cause a drop in the revenue.

Criteria for an ideal menu

- An ideal menu should satisfy guests by catering to their preferences for good food and beverage. To do this, the establishment should know the type of guests it is likely to serve.

- A menu should be compiled taking into account the season of the year, the capacity of the production staff and the capability of the service personnel.

- A menu should be compiled taking into consideration the type of establishment, especially the size of the kitchen and dining area, and the equipment available to both the production and service staff.

- The pricing of the dishes should be reasonable and based on the availability of fresh raw materials, calculated costs and revenue projections.

- A menu should be balanced with enough variety provided for guests to select the food of their choice. A menu should not be too long or too short. The quality of food should be standardised and should not differ in taste and appearance from day to day.

- Special care should be taken while catering to different religious and social communities for whom certain foods are taboo.

The trends in food and eating habits have changed drastically in recent years. Urban guests have access to more information from around the world. Business travel and travel for leisure have become more common, and guests have become more adventurous, so much so they are willing to try out new cuisines and different types of establishments.

Due to an increasing awareness among people about correct eating habits,a demand for health foods has increased, though local cuisine remains the most popular. In recent years, knowledge of what one eats, and the choices available, has grown to such an extent that eating establishments have sprung up offering delectable styles of cooking, presentation and tastes to satisfy the ever growing demand.

Courses of a menu

The French classical menu comprises a number of courses. Each course has one particular type of dish easily identifiable as belonging to that course. In an Indian *a la carte* menu, the sequence is not fixed, and several dishes are served simultaneously. The sequence of service in a French classical menu is termed as *courses of a menu*. Most western styles of cuisine follow this pattern.

The courses of a menu may be divided as follows:

Hors d'oeuvre — *Appetizer*

This is a course aimed at stimulating the palate, and consists of small tasty dishes, using a large array of different items such as anchovies, olives, cheese and smoked fish. They are often referred to as *starters* or *appetizers*. This course could also include salads. Some examples of *hors d'oeuvre* are *Canapés*, *Quenell* and *Shrimp cocktail*.

Potage — *Soups*

In a French classical menu, the soup course follows the *hors d'oeuvre*. There are several varieties of soups, but it broadly includes clear (consommé) and thick soups like Cream Veloute or puree and bisque or broths. Some examples of soups are *Consommé Celestine*, *Crème Dubary*, *Minestrone* and *Scotch Broth*.

Oeufs — *Eggs*

The omelette is the most popular item, but there are other styles of cooking and preparation of eggs such as boiled, en cocotte, poached or scrambled. This course is not included in the dinner menu. Some examples are *Omelette, Espagnole, Oeuf en Cocotte a la crème, Oeuf poche florentine.*

Farinaceous/Farineaux — *Pasta*

This is Italy's contribution to the courses of the menu. It includes different kinds of pasta such as spaghetti, lasagne and gnocchi. Pasta is made from durum semolina or milled durum wheat to which water is added to form a dough. It can be coloured and flavoured in various ways. There are more than 200 varieties of pasta. The ingredients, size, shape and colour determine the type of pasta. Some examples could include *Spaghetti Bolognaise, Lasagne Napolitaine* and *Macaroni au gratin.*

Poisson — *Fish*

The next course is the fish course. It includes shellfish and sea and fresh water fish. They are cooked in different styles such as poached, grilled, baked, shallow and deep fried. Some examples could include *Fish Meuniere, Lobster Americaine* and *Grilled Prawns.*

Entrée — *The first meat course*

It usually comprises a dish made up of steak, cutlets, casseroles or stews. Some examples are *Steak au poirre, Veal cutlets* and *Irish stew.*

Sorbet — *The rest course*

Sorbet is intended as a pause or rest course in a long meal. It refreshes the palate with a water-ice. Sorbet is a water-ice served with Italian meringue that is flavoured with champagne or a liqueur. Some examples are *Sorbet Italian* and *Sorbet crème de menthe.* Russian or Egyptian cigarettes are often passed around during this course.

Relêve — *The second meat course*

This includes large joints of meat such as a rib of beef, a joint of lamb, mutton or pork. Nowadays this course is often included in the *entrèe.* Some examples are *Crown roast, Roast loin of pork* and *Braised saddle of lamb.*

Rôti — *Roast*

This course normally consists of game or poultry and is often included in the *entrèe.* Each dish is accompanied with its own particular sauce and salad. Some examples are *Roast chicken, Braised duck* and *Roast quail.*

Légumes — *Vegetables*

These can be served separately as an individual course or may be included along with the *entrèe, relêve* or *roast* courses. Some examples are *Cauliflower mornay, Baked jacket potato* and *Grilled tomatoes.*

Entrêmet — *Sweet*

This could include hot or cold sweets, gateaux, soufflés or ice-cream. Some examples are *Apple pie, Chocolate soufflé* and *Cassata ice-cream.*

Fromage — *Cheese*

This is an alternative to the outdated savoury course, and may be served before or after the sweet course. It is usually served with butter, crackers and occasionally celery. *Gouda, Camembert* and *Cheddar* are some examples of cheese.

Desserts — *Fresh fruit and nuts*

This is the fruit course usually presented in a basket and placed on the table, as part of the table decor, and served at the end of the meal. All forms of fresh fruit and nuts may be served in this course.

Beverage — *Coffee*

This is not a course, but may be offered at the end of a meal, and may include different varieties of coffee such as *filter, cappucino* and *Cona coffee.*

The sequence discussed above may be used to compile and present *menus* for both, an *a la carte* restaurant as well as in catering for a function or special party. Beverage is usually an addition and not taken into account when counting the courses.

SUMMARY

1. The menu originated from the bill of fare and has since then served a practical purpose in catering.
2. Menus have several uses in the catering industry, and are an important aspect of a caterer's work.
3. An ideal menu should satisfy guests by catering to their preferences for good food and beverage.
4. The two main types of menus are *a la carte* which means *from the card* and *table d'hôte* meaning *from the table of the host.*
5. The sequence of courses in a French classical menu is internationally known as *courses of the menu.* They are *hors d'oeuvre, potage, oeufs, pasta, fish, entrèe, sorbet, relevê, rôti, légumes, entrémet, fromage, desserts* and *beverage.*

Review Questions

Answer the following questions :

1. Define the term menu, its origin and role in catering.

2. Explain briefly the different types of menus.

3. What does planning a menu mean?

4. List the criteria for an ideal menu.

5. Define nouvelle cuisine and explain its evolution.

6. Name and explain the courses in a French classical menu. Give two examples for each course.

Projects

1. *Compile different a la carte menus for all outlets in a luxury hotel taking into consideration the criteria for an ideal menu.*

2. *Plan five table d'hôte menus using the courses of the French classical menu as a guideline.*

3. *Plan a popular menu for banquets selecting dishes commonly served in Indian luxury hotels.*

Glossary

A la carte : A multiple choice menu with each dish being priced separately.

Bill of fare : A menu.

Cooked to order : The dish will only be cooked after the order has been received in the kitchen.

Cracker : A thin flaky dry biscuit, usually eaten with cheese.

Fixed menu : Another term for a *table d'hôte* menu.

French classical menu : Each course identified as belonging to a particular course that follows a sequence of service.

Health food : Natural food(s) with no chemical additives.

Menu : A list of items that are available in a restaurant. An important document used as a selling tool and an important aspect of budgetary control.

Menu planning : The putting together of a list of dishes with their prices by a caterer.

Nouvelle cuisine : A type of French cuisine, which advocates the use of absolutely fresh ingredients and light sauces without the addition of flour as a thickening agent.

Revenue projection : Forecasting earnings using the correct formula.

Table d'hôte : A fixed number of courses comprising the whole meal at a fixed price.

Water-ice : Frozen water flavoured with fruit juice and sugar, served as a dessert.

9

Food and Accompaniments

■■■■■■■■■■■■■■■■■■■■■■■■■■■■■■

> **Objectives :** A study of this chapter would enable you to :
> ◇ *Understand why accompaniments are served along with food.*
> ◇ *Identify the standard accompaniments and cover for selected dishes.*
> ◇ *Specify the categories under which cheese can be classified.*
> ◇ *Name the popular varieties of cheese from different parts of the world.*

Accompaniments are generally *flavoured foods or sauces offered with specific dishes*. They should not be confused with a garnish, which in most cases is an integral part of a dish and is always served from the kitchen. Appropriate accompaniments enhance the flavour of a dish by providing a balance or contrast to its taste. For example, rich food may attain a balance when accompanied by an appropriate sauce or the taste of bland food may improve when accompanied by a pickle or a *chutney*. If accompaniments are matched correctly with a dish, it brings about a little extra appreciation of the meal and adds to the diner's delight.

Accompaniments can be served in sauce-boats, small bowls or dishes, on plates or in bottles and jars.

Accompaniments help to :

• Enhance the *flavour* of food, for example, pickle for Indian food.

• *Moisten* the food, for example, mint *chutney* for *tandoori* chicken.

- Enhance the *nutritive value* of a dish, for example, sage, onion and mince stuffing in roast turkey.

- Provide *contrast in taste,* for example, mustard for roast beef.

- Provide *colour* to the food, for example, hollandaise sauce for hot asparagus.

- Give a *name to a dish,* for example, bolognaise sauce gives Spaghetti Bolognaise its name.

A selection of dishes with their standard accompaniments and the cover required for each dish is given in the *appendix.*

Cheese

The history of cheese making goes back to the earliest livestock farmers, who used to let milk curdle, then beat it with branches, press it on stones and let it dry in the sun. They then sprinkled it with salt. This was an ideal way of converting excess milk into a form that could be stored.

Over the centuries, techniques improved in the manufacturing of cheese and this led to a great variety of cheese. Thus regional characteristics of various kinds of cheese emerged and were associated with the place from where they were made.

Cheese is a very nutritious dairy product relished by people all over the world. It is made from coagulated milk, cream, skimmed milk, or a mixture of any of these. When eaten at the end of a meal it prevents dental cavities because of its alkaline content.

The texture of cheese depends on the maturation period. Cheese is a course in the French classical menu and is served after the *entrêmet* course. It is usually accompanied with butter, crackers and occasionally celery.

The recognised categories of cheese are :

i. *Fresh*   ii. *Semi-hard*   iii. *Soft*   iv. *Hard*   v. *Blue*

Varieties of cheese

Brie : This is a soft creamy cheese from France which has an edible white surface mould. It is always in the shape of a disc.

Camembert : This is a strong, pungent and soft French cheese. It is made in Normandy from the milk of cows, goats and sheep.

Roquefort : This is an extraordinarily delicate and subtle natural French cheese, made out of ewe's milk. It has blue veins running through it. The maturing takes place in caves. The humidity in the caves causes the veining.

Cheddar : A natural, hard English cheese which ranges from mild and mellow to rich and nutty. It is also the most widely imitated cheese and is made all over the world.

Stilton : A classic English cheese which is available in both white and blue varieties. White Stilton possesses less flavour than the blue. Blue Stilton is a velvety, close textured, unpressed cheese with a smooth, creamy white to pale ivory paste, marbled with a network of greenish-blue veins.

Caerphilly : Originally made in Wales, this cheese is now made all over Britain. It is a semi-hard buttermilk-flavoured cheese.

Mozzarella : This is one of the best known Italian cheeses. It is a soft, white, bland tasting cheese used on pizzas because of its stretchability and quick melting properties.

Gorgonzola : This is a type of rich cheese with bluish-green veins.

Parmesan : This classical Italian cheese is hard and crumbly with a grainy texture, a sharp aroma and piquant flavour. It is grated and sprinkled on pasta and other Italian dishes.

Edam : This is a natural semi-hard Dutch cheese which is shaped like a cannon ball with a unique coating of red wax. This cheese is a family favourite all over the world as it has excellent keeping qualities.

Gouda : This semi-hard Dutch cheese with a mild buttery flavour and a yellow wax rind, accounts for two-thirds of the cheese produced in Holland.

Gruyère : A semi-hard Swiss cheese which has a sweet, dry flavour with a nutty aftertaste. The rind is reddish brown and is known for the pea-sized holes on its surface.

Emmenthal : A hard cheese with a sweet, dry flavour in which the crust is discarded.

Cream or cottage : This is an unripened fresh cheese which has its origin in the USA. It is known as *paneer* in India. It is made from skimmed milk and is very low in fat content. This cheese is generally unpressed, lightly moulded and salted.

Service of cheese

Cheese should be served from a cheeseboard with a separate cheese knife for each variety. The service personnel should know the names, types and flavours of different varieties of cheese.

SUMMARY

1. Accompaniments are flavoured foods and sauces served along with a dish or a meal. They enhance the flavour of a dish and balance its taste.

2. Different courses of a menu have different accompaniments.

3. Accompaniments are universally accepted as standard but may vary in some parts of the world.

4. Cheese is a dairy product made from coagulated milk, cream, skimmed milk or a mixture of all three.

5. Cheese can be categorised as fresh, soft, semi-hard, hard and blue.

Review Questions

Answer the following questions :

1. Describe the role accompaniments play when served with a dish or a meal.

2. Name the standard accompaniments and cover for two items each from hors d'oeuvre, the meat course and poultry.

3. When is cheese served in a French classical menu and why?

4. Name any three varieties of cheese.

Projects

1. *Identify any two internationally popular dishes and write their appropriate accompaniments and cover.*

2. *Make a chart showing the different varieties of cheese with their prominent characteristics.*

Glossary

Blinis : A small savoury pancake, Russian in origin and made from leavened bread.

Chipolata : A small sausage about 2 centimetres in diameter, made from coarsely chopped sausage meat.

Chestnut puree : Boiled and sieved chestnuts made into a sauce.

Cranberry sauce : A sauce made from a red berry. It is a traditional accompaniment to roast turkey.

Crouton : A small piece of fried or toasted bread served with a soup or used as a garnish.

Crackers : Thin flaky dry biscuits typically eaten with cheese.

English mustard : A yellow condiment which consists of a mixture of black and white mustard. It is sold in fine powdered form. It should be mixed with water before service.

French mustard : A pungent mustard sold in the form of a paste. It is made from black or brown mustard seeds. Dijon, a town in France is famous for its French mustard.

Grilled flute : A thin slice of French bread weighing about 100 grams which is grilled before service.

Hollandaise sauce : A creamy sauce of melted butter, egg yolks and vinegar. It is usually served with fish.

Horseradish sauce : It is made from the root of the horseradish plant. It is grated, boiled, reduced, strained and finished with mustard and egg yolks.

Melba toast : Very thin slices of bread with one side of the crust cut, before it is toasted.

Mixed grill : An assortment of grilled meat such as chicken, beef, sausage and topped with a fried egg.

Mayonnaise : A thick creamy sauce made with egg yolks, oil and vinegar used especially on cold foods such as salads.

Mulligatawny soup : A soup of Indian origin, flavoured with curry powder and spices.

Pate de foie gras : Pate made from the liver of a fattened goose.

Pepper mill : An implement that grinds whole pepper corns, when the handle is turned.

Redcurrant jelly : A jelly made from redcurrant berries, traditionally served with roast mutton.

Stuffing : To fill the interior of poultry and joints of meat with an appropriate mixture. The ingredients used give the name to the stuffing.

Underliner : A side plate or saucer with a doily paper on which a variety of items are served.

Vinaigrette : A cold sauce made from vinegar, oil, pepper and salt. It is used mainly as a dressing for salads.

Yorkshire pudding : A British speciality made from a batter of flour, eggs and milk which is then baked in an oven. It is a traditional accompaniment to roast beef.

10

Know your Beverages

■■■■■■■■■■■■■■■■■■■■■■■

> **Objectives :** A study of this chapter would enable you to :
> ✧ *Understand the process of manufacturing beer and to identify the various types of beer.*
> ✧ *Identify different types of spirits such as whisky, brandy, rum, gin, vodka and tequila.*
> ✧ *Identify the types of whisky and describe the process of manufacturing whisky.*
> ✧ *Discuss what is meant by a liqueur and list its predominant characteristics and places of origin.*

Beer

Beer is available in all bars in one form or the other, and is classified as an alcoholic beverage. The alcoholic content of beer is low. It is usually between 3 to 8 per cent. The ingredients used in the manufacture of beer are *malted barley, sugar, hops* and *water*. Any cereal containing starch such as maize, rice, corn or wheat can also be used to make beer. However, barley is used often, as the conversion of sugar into alcohol by brewer's yeast is not so easily accomplished in other cereals. Hops give beer its bitterness, pleasant aroma and a fine froth.

The process of manufacturing beer

Brewing

For interest
The first technical book on beer was published in 1595 by Tadeas Hajek from Czechoslovakia.

Crushed malted barley is mixed with warm water. The solution that is obtained from this brew is called *wort*. The wort is cooled to 16°C in a refrigerator. This process takes about 10-12 hours.

Fermentation

A special strain of yeast called *brewer's yeast* is added to the *wort* for fermentation. The yeast breaks down the sugar in the malt to produce *alcohol* and *carbon-dioxide*. This stage lasts for 10-12 days.

Maturing

At this stage *finings,* a clarifying agent is added to clarify and brighten the fermented beer by attracting the sediment to the bottom of the cask. The most common clarifying agent used is *isinglass* — a product obtained from the bladder of the sturgeon fish. A solution of sugar and hops called *priming* is also added to improve the condition of the beer. The beer is then left to mature in casks for 3 to 4 months.

Racking

Racking is a process of *running off* the beer from one cask to another so as to leave the sediment behind.

Filtration

After racking, the beer is stored in *refrigerated wooden casks* for 6 months. It is then filtered and bottled. The beer acquires its colour from the wooden casks.

Beer should be served cold, with a fine collar of froth or head on it. The froth comes from the introduction of carbon-dioxide. Beer mugs should be washed properly to avoid grease as it reduces the froth. Beer is an all season beverage. It is specially savoured in summer.

Types of beer

Lager : The word *lager* means *to store.* Lager beer is stored in refrigerated vats for 6 months during the maturation stage.

Pilsner lager : These are bottom fermented light-coloured beers derived from the Czech original. They were earlier stored during maturation in the limestone caves of Pilsen, a small town in Czechoslovakia.

Ale : This beer is slightly cloudy and hoppy to taste and traditionally served at room temperature. It has a moderate alcoholic content of 3.5 to 6 per cent.

Porter : It is a fairly dark beer with a strong malt flavour, caused due to the malt being roasted for a long period. It gets its name from the porters of London who were known to favour this beer. It emits a reddish halo when placed in front of a source of light.

Stout : It is dark in colour, very dry and fairly bitter in taste, due to a strong hoppy flavour. The best known variety is *Irish stout* or *Guinness.*

Draught : This beer is filled in sterilized kegs and is allowed to mature in the cellars before it is sold for consumption. Draught beer cannot be stored for a long time, as secondary fermentation takes place in the cask itself.

Beer is sold in bottles and cans, as it retains a consistent flavour and stays in good condition for a reasonable length of time.

Some popular kinds of beer from around the world
American ...... *Budweiser, Coors*
Australian ..... *Fosters*
English .... *Pale Ale, Fuller's London Pride, Porter, Mc Ewan's Scotch Ale*
Irish .... *Guinness Stout*
German......... *Pils Export, Weizenbier*
Dutch .... *Heineken*
Japanese .... *Kirin*
Belgian.......... *Chimay, Duvel, Gueuze, Lambic*
Indian .... *Kingfisher, United Breweries (U.B), Kalyani Black Label, Haywards, London Pilsner*

Spirits

All spirits are produced by distilling fermented beverages in **stills**. *A still is an apparatus used in the distillation of alcoholic beverages.* Stills have been in existence for over 400 years. The process of distillation is based on the principle that ethyl alcohol vaporises at a lower temperature (78°C) than water. There are two main methods of producing spirits. They are the **pot-still** method and the **patent** or **continuous still** *(coffey)* method.

The different materials used in the manufacture of some common spirits are :

• Barley, maize or rye to make *whisky, gin* and *vodka.*

• Grape wine to make *brandy.*

• Molasses to make *rum.*

• Pulque *(Pulp of the Agave Tequilana)* to make *tequila.*

Whisky

Whisky is a spirit obtained by the distillation of the fermented mash of grain usually barley, maize or rye or a mixture of all three in different proportions. It is then aged in wooden casks. The word *whisky* gets its name from its Gaelic variations namely, *Usquebaugh or Uisgebeathe* which means *strong waters*. It should be noted, that the Scottish water plays an important role in giving Scotch its special taste.

Two types of whiskies are mixed to produce Scotch. They are *malt whisky* which gives Scotch its body and character and *grain whisky* which is used for its lightness. Both are blended to give Scotch whisky its unmistakable taste.

Malt whisky : A blend of whiskies from different casks and of various ages, but from the same malt distillery is called *single malt whisky* or *pure malt whisky*.

Grain whisky : This whisky is a product of a mixture of malted and unmalted barley which is crushed, fermented and distilled.

Blended whisky : This whisky is a blend of both malt and grain whiskies.

Whisky making process

- Barley is soaked in water for a few days and then spread on a concrete floor to germinate for 8-12 days.

- It is then subjected to heat over fires of smokeless coal and peat. The smoke given out by the peat gives an aroma to the malt.

- The ground malt is crushed with hot water to produce a sweetish liquor called *wort*.

- This *wort* is cooled and then fermented by yeast which converts the sugar into a crude alcohol called *wash*.

- The *wash* is distilled twice in a pot-still by heating. As alcohol has a lower boiling point than water, it vaporises faster. It is then cooled and condensed back into liquid or pure whisky.

- This new whisky is poured into oakwood casks, where it is matured into a pleasant mellow spirit for as long as 15 years. *(By law, whisky should be allowed to mature for a minimum period of 3 years. Whisky loses its volume on storing due to evaporation)*.

- After the malt whisky and grain whisky are matured, they are blended or *married* to get the right quality.

- After blending, it is poured into casks, to further mature. To achieve its peak quality, whisky should be allowed to mature for a minimum period of 8 years.

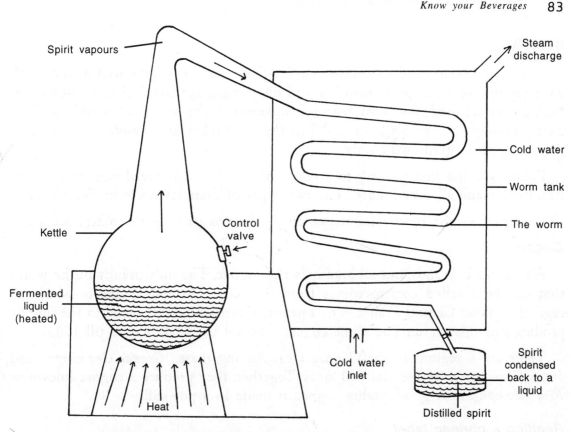

Fig. 10.1 *Pot-still method used in the manufacture of whisky*

Different kinds of whiskies are labelled under different brands. Each brand has certain differences based on its individual character and taste.

Some popular brands of whisky	
Scotch	: *Royal Salute, Chivas Regal, White Horse, Vat 69, Johnny Walker (Red and Black Labels)*
Bourbon	: *Old Grand Dad, I.W.Harper*
Canadian	: *Canadian Club*
Irish	: *Old Bushmills, Jamesons*
Indian	: *Royal Challenge, Peter Scot, Single Malt*

The main whisky producing countries and the types of whisky produced are :

Scotland .... *Scotch Whisky*

Ireland .... *Irish Whisky*

United States of America .... *Bourbon*

Canada .... *Canadian Club*

Brandy

Brandy can be defined as a spirit distilled from wine. It is produced in almost all wine producing areas, by fermenting and distilling grape juice. When fruits other than grapes are used, the word *brandy* is linked with the name of the fruit, such as cherry brandy and apricot brandy. When the label reads just *brandy,* it means that it is made from grape wine only.

France was the first country to produce brandy for widespread commercial sale. Brandy is made all over France. The two types of brandies made in France are :

    i. *Cognac* — the most famous brandy.   ii. *Armagnac* — the oldest brandy.

Cognac

All cognac is brandy, but all brandy is not cognac. The only brandy in the world that can be labelled cognac comes from the Charente and Charente Maritime regions in West Central France. The town of Cognac lends its name to the brandy produced in this region.The name cognac was not used for brandy till 1783.

There are 6 regions in the Cognac area. Among these, *Grande Champagne* and *Petite Champagne* are the classical areas. Together, they produce a cognac known as *Fine Champagne.* A good quality cognac is made in a pot-still.

Reading a cognac label

The *longer* a brandy matures in the cask before bottling, the *finer* is the quality and the *higher* is its price. The letters on a label indicate the number of years a brandy has been matured. The minimum age of maturation for the youngest cognac is 4 years while the average age is 10 to 15 years.

The letters *VSOP* on a label mean *Very Superior Old Pale.* It indicates that the cognac is original and not darkened or flavoured with additives. The letters *VSEP* or *XO* mean *Very Superior Extra Pale* or *Extraordinarily Old* respectively. These letters on a label indicate that the cognac has been aged for a much longer period. If the letters *VS (Very Superior)* or *VSP (Very Superior Pale)* or three stars ★ ★ ★ appear on the label, it indicates that the minimum period of maturation of the cognac is 2 years.

When a cognac is labelled with a special name such as *Napoleon, Cordon Bleu, Triomphe, XO* or *Extra Anniversaire,* it means that the minimum maturation age is 6 years but may run to an average age of 20 years. The cognac with the word *Napoleon* on its label, pays tribute to General Napoleon Bonaparte, who was reported to have been fond of drinking cognac.

Some popular brands of cognac are *Courvosier, Hennessy, Martell* and *Remy Martin.*

Armagnac

The name *armagnac* is given to the brandy made in the Armagnac region of South-West France. It is the world's oldest brandy. It predates cognac by about two centuries and is being brewed continuously for over 500 years. However, the total production of armagnac is less than 10 per cent of that of cognac. Armagnac type of brandy also uses a similar system of stars, letters and names on its labels as cognac to indicate levels of age and quality and is subject to similar regulations. A minor difference is that for the Napoleon category of armagnac, the minimum age of maturation for the youngest brandy in the blend is 5 years whereas cognac requires 6 years.

Some popular brands of armagnac are *Hors d' age (BA), Reserve de Moines (BA), Napoleon XO (BA)* and *Janneau*.

Vodka

This is a highly rectified patent-still spirit. It is purified by passing through activated charcoal which removes all the aroma and flavour. It can be described as a colourless and flavourless spirit.

Vodka is essentially a neutral spirit which can be distilled from anything fermentable including potatoes, but most vodkas are made from grain. Vodka does not require maturation.

Some popular brands of vodka	
American :	*Smirnoff de Czar, Popov, Reiska, Wolfschwidth*
Russian :	*Stolichnaya, Moskovaya*
Polish :	*Wybonowa Wodka*
Indian :	*Czar Alexander, Romanov*

Gin

The term *gin* is taken from the first part of the French word *Genièvre* which means *juniper*. Juniper is the main flavouring agent used in the production of gin.

Manufacture of gin

High proof spirits are first distilled from grain. They are then redistilled with juniper berries, peels of citrus fruits, bark of cassia, root of angelica, anise, coriander seeds and botanicals *(flavouring agents)*. Like vodka, gin does not require aging. Depending on the botanicals used, gin may have a herbal, flowery or woody taste. Each distillery has its own closely guarded formula for the type and proportion of flavourings used in its gin.

Some popular brands of gin		
British	:	*Beefeater, Plymouth, Tanqueray*
American	:	*Gilbeys, Gordons, Hiram Walker*
Indian	:	*Blue Riband, Booths, Mansion House*

Rum

Rum is a spirit manufactured by fermenting and distilling molasses, a by-product of sugar. It is believed that the word *rum* is derived from *Saccharums* which means *sugar* or *beet*. There are two kinds of rum, *white* and *dark*.

White rum is dry, light and vodka-like. It is aged in wooden casks for a minimum of 1 year and filtered before bottling to remove its colour.

Dark or *amber* rum is fuller and more aromatic than the white rum. Caramel is added before bottling to achieve the desired shade and to slightly enhance the flavour.

Some popular rum-producing countries are Puerto Rico, Jamaica, Cuba, Trinidad, Barbados, Guyana and the Bahamas.

Some popular brands of rum	
Dark Jamaican	: *Appleton Punch, Myers Original Rum, Lemon Hart, Jamaica*
White Jamaican	: *Appleton White*
Puerto Rican	: *Captain Morgan, Myers Golden Rich*
Indian	: *Khodays XXX, Old Monk*

Tequila

This is a Mexican spirit made by fermenting and distilling the juice of the blue Agave Tequilana plant. The spirit gets its name from the town of Tequila, situated in West-Central Mexico. It is available in three styles.

White or *silver label tequila* is colourless and requires little or no aging.

Gold label tequila undergoes some amount of aging in used barrels, which softens it. The addition of caramel gives it a straw-gold colour.

Anejo or *aged tequila* is smoother and more mellow than the other tequilas, as it is aged for 1 to 3 years in wood.

Traditionally tequila is drunk neat, preceded by a lick of salt and followed by a bite into a lemon wedge. An alternative is to follow tequila with *sangria*, a seasoned tomato and orange juice mixture.

Some popular brands of tequila are *Cuervo 1800, Pepe Hopez* and *Jose Cuervo*.

| **Other varieties of spirits** |

Aquavit : This spirit is manufactured in Scandinavia from potatoes or grain, and is flavoured with herbs such as caraway seeds. Aquavit should be served chilled.

Arrack : Arrack is made from the sap of palm trees. It is mainly produced in India, Sri Lanka, Java and Jamaica.

Eau de vie : This is the fermented and distilled juice of fruits which is mainly produced in Europe. Some varieties of Eau de vie are :

Kirschwasser from cherries — Germany   *Slivovitz from plums* — Yugoslavia

Mirabelle from plums — France   *Framboise from strawberries* — France

Poire William from pears — Switzerland and Alsace   *Fraise from strawberries* — France

Grappa : It is an Italian brandy distilled from the fermented residue of grapes after they have been pressed in wine making.

Kirsch : This is a colourless spirit distilled from the fermented juice of cherries. It goes well with pineapple and is mainly produced in Germany and Switzerland.

Sake : This is a Japanese rice wine and is usually drunk luke warm.

Schnapps : It is a spirit produced from grain or fermented potato base and flavoured with caraway seeds. It is produced mainly in the Netherlands, Germany and Scandinavia.

Liqueurs

A liqueur or a cordial is an alcoholic beverage, prepared by combining a spirit (usually brandy) with certain flavourings called *botanicals*. All liqueurs require a spirit-base such as brandy, rum or a neutral spirit. Flavouring ingredients such as aniseed, caraway seeds, wormwood, nutmeg, cherries, apricots, cinnamon and the rind of citrus fruit are commonly used.

The two basic methods of making liqueurs are :

- *Heat* or *infusion method* : In this method pot-stills are used for distillation. The high temperature helps in extracting the oils and flavours from herbs, peels and roots.
- *Cold* or *maceration method* : In this method, the flavour is obtained by soaking soft fruit in brandy in oak casks for a long period of time.

Liqueurs are natural digestives. They are sweet, potent and contain important herbal oils. Hence they are usually served as after-dinner drinks. They are used in cocktails and desserts, as frappés *(served by pouring over crushed ice)* and as fillings in chocolates.

Two of the oldest liqueurs are *Chartreuse* and *Benedictine*. The letters *DOM* on a Benedictine bottle means *Deo Optimo Maximo* — *To God most good, most great.*

Some liqueurs and their predominant colours and flavours

Liqueurs	Colour	Flavour/Spirit Base	Country
Aquavit	White	Caraway/Spirit	Denmark
Benedictine	Yellow/Green	Herbs/Brandy	France
Cointreau	Clear	Orange/Brandy	France
Chartreuse	Green	Herbs/Brandy	France
Creme de Cacao	Brown/Clear	Cocoa beans/Rum	France
Creme de menthe	Green	Mint/Brandy	France
Grand Marnier	Amber	Orange/Brandy	France
Drambuie	Golden	Honey, herbs/Whisky	Scotland
Kahlua	Pale chocolate	Coffee/Rum	Mexico
Sambuca	Clear	Liquorice/Spirit	Italy
Tia Maria	Brown	Coffee/Rum	Jamaica

SUMMARY

1. Beer is a popular alcoholic beverage made from malted barley, sugar, hops and water.

2. The various stages in making beer are brewing, fermenting, maturing, racking and filtration.

3. The different types of beers made around the world are : lager, pilsner, ale, porter, stout and draught.

4. All spirits are produced by the distillation of fermented beverage in pot or patent-stills.

5. Whiskies are classified as malt, grain or blended. Scotch whisky is the best known whisky.

6. Brandy is the spirit distilled from wine. France produces both cognac and armagnac types of brandies which are famous all over the world.

7. Vodka is a highly rectified patent-still spirit.

8. Gin is flavoured with juniper berries.

9. Rum is made by fermenting and distilling molasses while tequila is made by fermenting and distilling the juice of the blue Agave Tequilana plant.

10. A liqueur is an alcoholic beverage prepared by combining a spirit with certain flavourings called botanicals. Liqueurs are natural digestives.

Review Questions

Answer the following questions :

1. Explain how beer is manufactured and name the different types of beer.

2. Explain the whisky making process.

3. Distinguish between malt whisky and grain whisky.

4. Write short notes on :   i. Vodka   ii. Gin   iii. Rum
5. Distinguish between cognac and armagnac type of brandies.
6. What is a liqueur? Name six liqueurs with their principal flavours and countries of origin.

Projects

1. *Identify six international brands of beer, whisky, cognac, rum, vodka and tequila and list their countries of origin.*
2. *Visit a brewery/distillery in your city and make a report of your observations.*

Glossary

Botanicals : Flavouring agents used in aromatized wines, some spirits and liqueurs.

Carbonated : A liquid impregnated with carbon dioxide to make it fizzy.

Collar (head) : The froth on top of a glass of beer.

Crushed malt : Crushed barley from which beer is made.

Distillation : The process of converting a fermented beverage into a spirit by passing it through a pot-still.

Fermentation : The breakdown of a substance by micro-organisms such as yeast and bacteria usually in the absence of oxygen. For example, the breakdown of sugar to ethyl alcohol in making beers, wines and spirits.

Frappé : A liqueur served by pouring over crushed ice.

Finings (Isinglass) : A product obtained from the bladder of the sturgeon fish which is added to beer to clarify and brighten it.

Infusion : The liquid extract that results from steeping a substance in water.

Juniper : The principal flavouring agent used in the manufacture of gin.

Maceration : To soften or break down fruit by soaking it in a liquid for some time.

Molasses : Thick dark brown sugar produced when sugar is refined. It is used in the manufacture of rum.

Neat : Refers to liquor drunk without any mixes or ice.

Peat : A kind of turf used as a fuel in the manufacture of whisky.

Rectified spirit : A very pure spirit such as vodka.

Still (pot and patent) : An apparatus used in the distillation of alcoholic beverages.

Wort : Crushed malt and hot water that produces a sweetish liquor in the whisky making process.

Wash : Crude wort fermented by yeast which is converted into an unrefined alcohol.

11

Wines

■■■■■■

> **Objectives :** A study of this chapter would enable you to :
>
> ❖ *Understand the definition of wine.*
>
> ❖ *Describe the wine making process and the classification of wines.*
>
> ❖ *Identify the different varieties of grapes used in the making of wine.*
>
> ❖ *Name the main wine producing countries of the world.*
>
> ❖ *Explain the sequence of service of wine.*
>
> ❖ *Highlight the harmonious relationship between wine and food.*

Wine is an *alcoholic beverage obtained from the fermentation of the juice of freshly gathered grapes, the fermentation of which has been carried out in the district of its origin according to local tradition and practice.* Generally the term *wine* is used to refer to a wide variety of beverages, ranging from the most exquisite to the homemade variety. However, it is recognised internationally as an alcoholic beverage made from fermented grape juice.

History of wine making

There are many biblical references to the growing of vines and the production of wine. The first evidence of wine making dates back to 12000 years. Archaeologists have traced it to the year 2000 BC in the Mesopotamia and Nile valley. Egyptian wall paintings also show the main stages of wine production. Historical records also mention a list of wines stored in the royal cellars of Assyria (present day Iran) around 800 BC.

The development of wine production

Growing of vines was first introduced and spread by the Greeks, especially to countries bordering the Mediterranean Sea. The economy of the Mediterranean countries depended on the production of grapes, wheat and olives. The Romans concentrated on growing vines in one area rather than growing small quantities in many areas. In this way, a few provinces provided wine for the entire empire. Since there were constraints in transporting wine from one end of the empire to the other, new vineyards were developed in parts of Hungary, Germany, France and England. The breaking up of the Roman empire and the resulting disruption of trade, made it necessary for far flung colonies to become self-sufficient. Thus, there was a gradual spread of wine production in those areas where vine growing had been discouraged earlier.

Expansion of the wine trade

A significant expansion of trade and industry began around 1000 AD and the trade of wine was in the forefront of this growth. For the next three centuries, the wine business developed with the growth of trade. Ships sailed to Northern Europe and established fairs in the cities of the Netherlands and Northern France.

During the beginning of the 14th century and upto the middle of the 15th century, there was a decline in trade. However, it began to recover in the late 15th century. During the 17th century, the deterioration in the quality of Italian wines and the imposition of heavy duty on French wines, adversely affected their sales. The sale of relatively cheap and previously unknown wines increased. The growth of the British imperial power in the 19th century boosted the trade in wine and led to the import of South African and Australian wines. Wine production began to keep pace with the demand. The growth of the wine trade further accelerated in the 20th century with an increased interest in high quality French table wines because of their greater consumption and a speculative market. This in turn led to a rise in the price of wines.

The production of Italian wines also increased rapidly. Italy produces more wine than any other country in the world, while France is the second largest producer of wine. Today, many wine producing countries are aggressively marketing their wines to countries which previously did not have much of a wine drinking population. The development of good Australian, South African and Californian wines among others, has given a further impetus to the wine drinking trend in different countries of the world. These wines compare favourably with some of the best in the world both in terms of quality and popularity.

Around five to seven thousand million gallons of wine are produced every year all over the world. The major wine producing countries in the world are Italy,

France, Germany, Spain, Argentina, Chile, Czechoslovakia, Portugal, Poland, Bulgaria, England, Austria, the United States of America, Russia, former Yugoslavia, Romania, Greece, Canada, Switzerland, Hungary, South Africa, New Zealand, Brazil and Australia.

Grape-vines

The grape-vine is a very hardy plant. It can survive and produce fruit under the most extreme conditions. Although grapes can be grown under a wide variety of conditions, they do not always provide juice of the quality necessary to make potable wine.

Vines used for producing wine on a commercial basis need two types of climatic conditions.

- There should be adequate sunlight to ripen the grapes.
- The winter should be moderate, but sufficiently cool to give the plant a chance to rest and restore its strength for the growing and fruiting season.

The ripened grapes contain two of the most important ingredients necessary for making wine. One is *sugar,* which is present in the flesh of the fruit, and the other is *yeast,* which is found on its skin.

Stages in wine making

Crushing : The grapes are crushed, after removing their stalks. The product obtained from crushing grapes is called *must.* When the grapes are crushed, the skins burst and the sugar and the yeast mix together. The coating on the skin of grapes consists of tiny yeast cells. This coating is known as *bloom.* The yeast causes fermentation of the grape juice.

Pressing : At this stage, the juice is separated from the solid grape residue.

Fermentation : During fermentation, the yeast acts on the sugar in the juice and converts it into alcohol and carbon dioxide. This is natural fermentation and continues until all the sugar is consumed by the yeast to produce a very dry wine without any trace of sweetness or the yeast cells die without consuming all the sugar and the alcoholic content in the wine reaches 16 per cent. The presence of the unused sugar makes the wine sweet.

Controlled fermentation : The process of fermentation is controlled by adding alcohol to the wine at the appropriate time. This is known as *fortification of wine.*

Sulphuring : When wine stops fermenting, moulds such as *aceto bacter* begin to break down the alcohol and destroy it by producing a *vinegary liquid.* Wine which contains more than a certain level of vinegar (acetic acid) is not potable. The effect of these moulds is countered by adding sulphur dioxide to the *must* before fermentation starts. This is known as *sulphuring.* Care should be taken to add the correct quantity of sulphur dioxide, as too much of it imparts an unpleasant flavour to the wine.

Racking and fining : Some sediments sink to the bottom of the cask when wine is run off from the fermenting vats into storage casks. The wine is then transferred to a fresh storage cask, leaving behind some more sediments. To clear the wine of the cloudiness caused by the tiny dead yeast cells, the wine is fined by adding *isinglass* or the *white of an egg.*

Maturation : This refers to the process of gradual improvement that some wines undergo between the period of fermentation and consumption. Maturation is caused by chemical changes which soften and mellow the wine and make it less acidic.

Classification of wine

Wine may be classified into :
- Natural or still wine
- Sparkling wine
- Fortified wine
- Aromatized wine

Wines may be dry or sweet, depending on their sugar content. Their colour can also vary from *red, white* or *rosé. Sparkling wines* are *white* or *pink.*

Red wine is made from red grapes while *white wine* is made from white or red grapes whose skins are removed from the *must* before the wine absorbs their colour.

Rosé wines are produced in exactly the same way as white or red wines, except that during fermentation the skin is left a little longer to give a rosy tinge to the wine. The best known rosé wine is *Tavel* from the Rhône valley. Rosé wine is normally served chilled.

Natural or still wines

These are good quality wines which may or may not be a blend of wines from more than one vineyard. These include red, white or rosé wines which may be either dry or sweet. They are referred to as *natural* or *still wines* because they do not have carbon dioxide in them. The alcoholic content of these wines ranges between 14 and 16 per cent.

Some examples of natural or still wines	
White	: *Chablis (Burgundy), Château D'Yquem (Bordeaux)*
Red	: *Château Latour (Bordeaux), Beaujolais (Burgundy), Château Neuf-du-pape (Rhône)*
Rosé	: *Cabernet d' Anjou (Loire), Rosé Tavel (Rhône)*

Sparkling wines

Carbon dioxide is introduced into sparkling wines during secondary fermentation to make them fizzy. Champagne is the undisputed king of sparkling wines. Sparkling wines other than champagne are known as *Vin mousseux*. The alcoholic content of sparkling wines is less than 14 per cent. They are normally taken on festive occasions and are compatible with most dishes.

Some examples of sparkling wines
Dom Pérignon (France), *Asti Spumante* (Italy) and *Sekt* (Germany).

Fortified wines

These are wines that are strengthened by the addition of brandy (made from grapes), either during or after fermentation. They have an alcoholic content ranging from 15 to 21 per cent. These wines can be had before or after a meal.

Some examples of fortified wines	
Sherry (Spain)	: *usually taken as an apéritif before a meal*
Port (Portugal)	: *usually taken after a meal as a digestive.*
Marsala (Sicily)	: *usually taken as a dessert wine.*
Madeira (Portugal)	: *unlike other fortified wines, this wine is fortified with a spirit made from sugarcane.*

Aromatized wines

These wines are also known as *apéritif* wines. They are prepared by the addition or fortification of brandy or neutral spirits and blended to a set style. They are flavoured with herbs, bark, roots, flowers, quinine or other botanicals (flavouring agents). They are often served in a mix with other alcoholic beverages such as cocktails. The alcoholic content ranges from 15 to 55 per cent.

Some examples of aromatized wines
Vermouth, Dubonnet, Lillet, Byrhh, Cap Corse and *Bitters*.

Vermouth : It is made using a low quality wine base which is flavoured with a variety of botanicals such as wormwood, nutmeg, orange peel, cinnamon, angelica root, bitter almonds or cinchona bark.

Some examples of vermouth		
Dry	:	*Martini, Chambéry, Cinzano, Noilly Prat*
Sweet	:	*Martini rosso, Martini bianco, Cinzano bianco, Noilly Prat red, Punt e Mes, Cinzano red*

Dubonnet red or white : This wine from France is made from a base of either sweet red wine or white wine flavoured with quinine.

Lillet : This is a French white wine apéritif fortified with armagnac brandy.

Byrhh : This red wine flavoured with quinine and various herbs and fortified with brandy is made in France.

Cap corse : It is an apéritif from Corsica. It is wine based and flavoured with herbs and quinine.

Bitters : This aromatized wine has many varieties. They are :

Campari : It is a pink Italian apéritif. It is bitter-sweet to taste and has a slight flavour of orange peel and quinine.

Angostura : This is named after a town in Venezuela, but is now mainly produced in Trinidad. It is brownish red in colour and is used mainly as a flavouring agent.

Amer picòn : This is a black and bitter apéritif from France.

Fernet branca : This is from Italy and is similar to Amer picòn.

Underberg : This wine is from Germany and tastes like iodine.

Some famous grape varieties used in making wine

To appreciate good wine, one should know the various types of grapes used in wine making. Knowledge of these varieties will help identify wines, as many of them are labelled according to the type of grapes. Secondly, the distinctive characteristics of many of these grapes, contribute to the taste of a particular wine.

There are many varieties of grapes found in the wine producing regions of the world. The following are the important varieties :

Cabernet Sauvignon

This is considered to be one of the best red wine grape varieties in the world. It is used in combination with other Bordeaux grapes such as *Cabernet Blanc* and *Merlot* in the production of the classic red Bordeaux wines. This grape gives the red Bordeaux wine its depth, aroma, long lasting flavour and keeping qualities. It can be recognised by its deep colour, fruity flavour and the aroma of blackcurrants. Though this variety of grape is from Bordeaux in France, it has been successfully grown in California, Australia, South Africa and Chile.

Chardonnay

This variety is used mainly to produce the white Burgundies of France. It is also one of the three grape varieties used in the making of champagne. Some well known wines made from this variety of grape are *Chablis* and *Meursault*.

Chenin-Blanc

This variety is used to make dry to medium-sweet white wines in Loire (France), California, Australia and South Africa.

Gamay

This variety of grape is grown in Beaujolais. It is used to produce a red wine in France and California. The wine is light in character and low in alcoholic content, but has a striking fruity bouquet and a distinctive pinkish-purple colour.

Gewürztraminer

This variety of grape is used in Germany, Australia, California and the Alsace region of France for producing a slightly scented spicy white wine.

Grenache

This variety of grape is grown in the southern region of France, California and Australia. It produces a light, fruity red wine.

Merlot

In Bordeaux and California, this variety of grape is often blended with the Cabernet Sauvignon variety to produce a more rounded wine. The famous wines of Pommerol (a region in Bordeaux, France) such as Châteaux Pétrus are made from this variety.

Pinot Noir

This variety like Cabernet Sauvignon is considered to be one of the best varieties of grapes for making red wine. It is used to make the classical red wines of Burgundy such as Côte-de-Nuits and Côte-de-Beaune. Pinot Noir is also a constituent grape used in the making of champagne. It has a distinct aroma and is usually paler, with a more subtle taste than Cabernet Sauvignon.

Riesling

This variety of grape has a hardy, resilient character. It is considered to be the white equivalent of Cabernet Sauvignon. It is used to make wines in Germany, Alsace, California and Australia. Most Riesling wines are dry to medium dry, but in Germany, some of the finest sweet dessert wines are made from this variety.

Sauvignon Blanc

This grape is a constituent of the sweet white wines of Barsac and Sauternes in Bordeaux in France. It is used to make some fine wines such as Pouilly-Fumé and Sancerre in the Loire region of France under the name *Blanc Fumé*. French wines called Sauvignon are often light, dry white wines.

Zinfandel

This grape is unique to California and has a berry-like flavour and is used for producing mainly red and some rosé and white wines.

Some famous wine producing countries

Europe has the greatest concentration of wine producing countries in the world. It produces about three-quarters of the world's output, to which France and Italy contribute almost one-quarter each.

French wines

France is the second largest producer of some of the finest wines in the world. There are many regions in the country that produce a wide range of wines, each with its own unique character. French wines are divided into four categories. The category is printed on the label, either in large letters, just above the name of the wine, or in small letters, just below it.

Appellation d'Origine Contrôlée (AOC)

According to French law, all French wines should bear a label indicating their place of origin. This is a guarantee of authenticity for quality wines that come from a specific area. The use of district, parish or vineyard names is strictly controlled by the system of Appellation Contrôlée. For example, the label *Appellation Bordeaux Contrôlée* indicates that the wine is from the Bordeaux region.

The functions of the system are :

- To maintain the quality and prestige of French wines.
- To protect the producers of high quality wines against unscrupulous competitors, who deceptively use labels similar to those of the genuine producers.
- To protect the consumer from being deceived by fraudulent labelling. This is done by setting up a detailed legal statement of the wine entitled to bear a particular label.

The conditions of the legal statement are :

- The vines should be grown within a specified area.
- The grape variety used should be specified. If two or more varieties are blended their proportion should be mentioned.
- The maximum quantity of wine to be produced is controlled by the system. If the wine is produced in excess the surplus wine should be sold as *vin ordinaire* (house wine).
- The wine should be checked by wine tasters so that the quality of all the wine produced is consistent.

Vin Délimité de Qualité Supérieure (VDQS)

The label with these words means *wines of superior quality*. *VDQS* are wines which rank slightly below the AOC category and are produced from specified vineyards and districts. They are good second quality wines of France. They are produced from particular vines under strict regulations, have a minimum alcoholic strength and are known by a black symbol on the label, about the size of a postage stamp.

ESTATE BOTTLED   CHÂTEAU BOTTLED

XXUUII

XIOO

OO

VINTAGE YEAR

BRAND or CHÂTEAU NAME

APPELLATION FOR WHICH THE WINE QUALIFIES

REGION IN WHICH THE WINE WAS PRODUCED		WINE IS A PRODUCT OF FRANCE
	NAME AND ADDRESS OF SHIPPER	
NET CONTENTS OF BOTTLE		ALCOHOLIC CONTENT BY PER CENT OF VOLUME

Fig. 11.1 *Shows what to look for on a French wine label*

Vin de pays

These are regional or country wines ranking just below the *VDQS* variety. The variety of grapes used, its place of origin and the minimum alcoholic content of the wine are carefully defined and limited by the district committee. These wines are used by the French almost everyday and are a delight in their diversity.

Vins de Table

These are the table wines of France. They come from various wine producing regions and are carefully blended to maintain a consistent quality.

Wine producing regions in France

Bordeaux

Bordeaux produces about one-third of all the better quality wines of France. It produces both red and white wines. However, Bordeaux is known for its red wines though over 50 per cent of the wine produced here is white.

Burgundy

Burgundy is the English name for the French district of Bourgogne. This district produces some of the world's finest red and white wines. The wines produced in Burgundy are best known for their diversity. This is because of the different types of soil found here. Sometimes the variation in the soil is so great that in a large vineyard one may get entirely different types of wines. In addition, the time of harvesting of grapes and the period of fermentation of the wine also differ. These factors affect the end result to a large extent.

Other wine producing regions of France are *Graves, Loire, Beaune, Alsace* and *Côtes-du-Rhône*.

Champagne

Champagne is a region in France where the best known sparkling wines are made. They are also made in other regions of France and in other countries. However, wines made only in the Champagne region are classified as *champagne*. The first sparkling wines made their appearance in the 17th century. By early 19th century, champagne became synonymous with sparkling wine. Champagne is a white sparkling wine. Pink champagne is produced by mixing red and white wine. The soil in the Champagne region is chalky and ideal for good dry white wines. The gentle slope of the land is suitable for the ripening of the grapes and for free draining of the soil. The sparkle in the wine is caused by the secondary fermentation which takes place in the bottle.

Steps in the manufacture of champagne

Pressing : After harvesting, the grapes are pressed thrice in large presses. The juice obtained from the first pressing is of the best quality. This is fermented to make *champagne*. The second pressing is harder and the *must* produced is used for *blending*. The *must* produced after the third and final pressing is used to make *local wine* or is *distilled into brandy*.

Fermentation : Fermentation takes place in casks till most of the sugar is converted into alcohol. At the appropriate time, fermentation is stopped by lowering the temperature.

Racking : The wine is run off into fresh casks leaving behind the sediment in the old casks. This procedure is called *racking*. The wine is then fined by adding *gelatine*. This attracts the microscopic particles in the wine to the bottom of the cask, leaving the wine clear and bright. The wine is then left untouched till spring.

Blending : Blending is done with the wine made from grapes brought from different vineyards. It requires great skill and experience to create a wine of consistently good quality and a fine style non-vintage champagne.

Secondary fermentation : A small quantity of sugar syrup is added to the wine just before bottling to ensure secondary fermentation in the bottle. This activates the dormant yeast cells in the wine. The yeast cells convert the sugar into alcohol. French law insists that the wine should be allowed to undergo secondary fermentation for at least a year, but most firms keep the bottles for three years before *remuage*.

Remuage : The fermented wine is put into special racks called *púpitres*, where the bottles are tilted. It takes three months for the bottles to be completely tilted upside down and for the yeast cells to collect around the cork.

Degorgement : The yeast cells collected around the cork are removed by a process called *degorgement*. This is done by freezing the neck of the bottle, so that the deposit of yeast cells is frozen along with the wine. When the bottle is opened the ice plug shoots out of the bottle.

Dosage : A little wine is added to top up the bottle after degorgement. This addition is called *dosage* and determines the sweetness of the champagne in the bottle by the amount of sugar present in the *dosage*.

Aging : Theoretically, champagne is ready to drink after degorgement, but connoisseurs insist that the wine should be aged in the bottle for at least a year. This enables the dosage to blend well with the rest of the wine.

Some champagne styles	Sizes of champagne bottles
Brut, natur ...... Very dry	*Magnum,* a wine bottle twice the standard size.
Sec .... Medium dry	*Jeroboam,* four times the standard size.
Demi-sec .... Medium sweet	*Rehoboam,* six times the standard size.
Demi-doux....... Sweet	*Methuselah,* eight times the standard size.
Rich doux......... Very sweet	*Salamanzail,* twelve times the standard size.
	Balthazar, sixteen times the standard size.
	Nebuchadnezzar, twenty times the standard size.

Other wine producing regions of France are *Côtes-de-Beaune, Côtes-du-Rhône, Graves* and *Loire.*

Popular brands of wines from France
Red : *Château neuf-du-Pape, Château Latour, Château Haut Brion, Beaujolais, Graves, St. Emilion, Château Reve d'or, Château Montrosé* and *Nuits-Saint George.*
White: *Chablis, Mâcon Blanc, Méursault, Montrachet, Corton-Charlemagne, Pouilly-Fuissé* and *Pouilly Fumé.*
Champagne : *Moet et Chandon, Dom Pérignon, Veauve Cliquot, Pol Rogers, Piper Hiedsieck, Tattitinger and Mumms.*

German wines

The basins of the River Rhine and its tributaries are the major wine producing areas in Germany. The Rhine divides Germany into two zones — the first zone stretching from the Alps to the North Sea and the second zone covering the north-eastern part of Germany. In the first zone, quality wines are produced from an area where the River Marne flows into the Rhine. These wines are known as *Hock,* named after the village Hockheimer where they are produced. *Moselle* wines are produced in the second zone where the River Moselle joins the River Rhine. These wines are equal in quality to wines produced from the Hock region. Moselle wines are bottled in green bottles while Hock wines are bottled in brown bottles.

Pfalz in Germany produces *Steinwine*. It is the only wine in Germany which is not bottled in long thin bottles.

German white wines are more delicate in taste, rich in bouquet, sweet and less alcoholic than French white wines. The addition of sweetness is a fairly recent development since all the sugar is used up during fermentation and unfermented grape juice called *sus-reserve* is added at the end for sweetness.

Italian wines

Italian red wines are better known than white wines.

Italian wines are classified into three groups :

- *Denominazione Controllate e Garantita* are premier quality wines.
- *Denominazione di Origine Controllata* are second quality wines.
- *Denominazione Semplica* are ordinary wines.

Chianti, a red wine made in *Tuscany* is known all over the world. It is sold in round bottomed bottles, encased in a straw basket. Four varieties of grapes are blended to make this wine. To prolong the process of fermentation, more grapes of a similar quality are sun dried and added to it. This process called *Governo* is peculiar to *Chianti*.

Reserva, the best known wine is aged for at least 5 to 6 years in wood and has an alcoholic content of 12.5 per cent. Unlike *Chianti* which is sold in round bottomed bottles, *Reserva* is sold in brown bottles shaped like those used for Bordeaux wines.

Some well known Italian white wines are *Frescati*, *Est-Est-Est* and *Soave*. The Piedmont area is known for producing Italy's famous sparkling wine *Asti Spumante*.

Portuguese wines

Portugal produces *Port wine,* which is a fortified wine. It is normally taken after dinner as a digestive. Portugal also produces *Mateus Rosé* and *Lancers*. Both these wines have a slight sparkle and are fairly sweet. *Vinhos Verdes* or *green* wines are made from immature or green grapes.

Some port wines are *Roncao, Noxal LB Port, Fonseca* and *Cockburns*.

Spanish wines

Spain is well known for producing *sherry*, a fortified wine, which is taken as an apéritif. Sherry is the English name for the wine produced in the districts surrounding the town of Jerez de la Frontera in southern Spain. It was called *sack* until the 17th century. Sherry-like wine is produced in South Africa which is of a fairly good quality as compared to the original from Spain.

Solera system

This is the system used for blending sherry. A series of casks all containing a similar type of wine are arranged in groups, each group older than its predecessor. When wine is required from a particular solera for blending, it is taken from each cask in the oldest group. These casks are replenished with sherry from the next group of casks. By blending from the solera, a sherry can be produced to any degree of sweetness or colour.

The various types of sherry		
Manzanilla	:	*A very dry sherry.*
Fino	:	*A fine, highly fragrant wine which is normally dry.*
Amontillado	:	*A medium dry sherry.*
Oloroso	:	*A medium sweet sherry, but less fragrant than fino.*
Amoroso/Cream	:	*A sweet cream sherry.*
Brown	:	*A very sweet sherry.*
Some brands of sherry		
Harveys Bristol Cream	:	*A sweet sherry, drunk as a dessert wine.*
Sandeman	:	*A dry sherry.*
Dry Sac	:	*A dry sherry.*
Tio Pepe	:	*A dry sherry.*

Hungarian wines

Hungary produces *tokay*, a very famous dessert wine. Tokay is situated near the Russian border on the River Bodrog. Tokay is made by piling grapes high in a trough. The juice is extracted by the enormous weight of the grapes. It ferments very slowly as it contains a lot of sugar. Eventually it becomes a wine, low in alcohol and sweet and concentrated in flavour.

Others

California, Australia and South Africa produce fairly good wines.The quality of these wines has improved over the years. Switzerland, Austria, Yugoslavia, Russia, Canada and India also produce some average quality wines.

Indian wines

1. Sparkling : *Marquis de Pompadour*
2. Still wines : *Bosca Cabernet, Bosca Riesling, Golconda ruby/white and Grovers.*

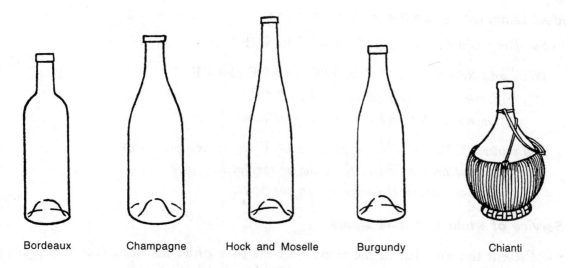

| Bordeaux | Champagne | Hock and Moselle | Burgundy | Chianti |

Fig. 11.2 *Shapes of wine bottles*

Service of wines

Wine and food should be matched and served at the *correct temperature* and in the *right manner*. The service of wine is a skill, and great care should be taken while serving the wine. The *wine waiter* or *sommelier*, is a person who has been specially trained to perform this exacting duty. A sommelier should possess extensive knowledge of all varieties of wines and food. He should be in a position to advise the guests about the wines available and the matching food that goes with them, or suggest to guests a wine to accompany the food that has been ordered. He should also know how to serve wine in a stylish and professional manner.

General rules for the service of wine

- Use the *appropriate glassware*. Red wines are served in a glass with a shorter stem, and white wines are served in a glass with a longer stem. The rounded sides and narrow top of the glassware trap the flavour and bouquet of a wine. A glass with a stem prevents the wine from getting warm through contact with one's palm.

- Glasses should be *spotlessly clean*. They should be rinsed in warm water. Detergent should not be used for washing as it kills the taste of the wine. A dry waiter's cloth should always be used to wipe glasses.

- Wine glasses should be placed on the *right hand side* of the cover.

- Wines should always be served at the *correct temperature*, so that guests appreciate the taste, bouquet and appearance of the wine.

Ideal temperature for the service of wine

Sparkling wines : 2°C to 8°C or 46°F to 54°F.

White and Rosé wines : 8°C to 12°C or 54°F to 64°F
- *Serve chilled, but not over chilled.*
- *Do not deep freeze a white or rosé wine.*

Red wines : 12°C to 18°C or 56°F to 66°F (room temperature)
- *Do not heat or warm the wine or the bottle.*
- *Do not disturb the sediment in the bottle.*

Service of white and rosé wines

- Present the wine list to the guest after the food order has been taken. Suggest a wine if necessary, keeping in mind the food that is to accompany it.

- When the guest has ordered the wine, place a white wine glass on the upper right-hand side of the water goblet.

- Inspect the wine in the cellar to see if the wine is the one ordered by the guest. Place it in a wine chiller three-fourths full of ice and a little water. Place the stand a little behind to the right of the host's chair and mount the wine chiller on the stand. Make sure the label of the bottle faces the guest. Drape a waiter's cloth over the bucket.

- Present the bottle to the guest to check if the temperature is suitable for service. Announce the name and year of vintage. Do not conceal the label, while presenting the bottle.

How to open a bottle of wine (carried out with the bottle in the wine chiller)

- Cut the foil below the lip of the bottle. Move the knife and not the bottle while doing so. Wipe the inside of the bottle and take it out of the wine chiller.

- Insert a cork screw, making sure that it does not go more than three-quarters through the cork. This is done to prevent its contact with the wine in the bottle.

- Draw the cork out slowly, and after a point gently pull out the cork to prevent it from breaking. Present the cork to the host on a quarter plate.

Fig. 11.3 *A wine chiller and stand*

- Wipe the mouth of the bottle with a clean napkin. Once the host has expressed satisfaction with the smell and feel of the cork, pour a small quantity of wine into the host's glass to taste. If approved, the host will give his assent to serve. If not, it should be replaced after ascertaining the reason for rejecting the wine.

Service of red wines

- Present the wine list to the guest.

- When the guest has ordered, place a glass with a shorter stem at the top right-hand side of the water goblet.

- Place the following items on the side station :

  - Wine cradle
  - Quarter plate
  - Napkin
  - Wine opener
  - Waiter's cloth
  - Knife

- Inspect and present the bottle to the guest resting it on the inside of the forearm on a waiter's cloth folded lengthwise. Display the label and announce the name and year of vintage of the wine.

- Once the guest has approved, place the bottle in the *wine cradle (a basket that holds a bottle of red wine during service).*

- Place the bottle on the side station. Cut and remove the foil, wipe the neck of the bottle and remove the cork. Place the cork on a quarter plate and present it to the guest for approval and place the bottle in the wine cradle.

- Pour a little wine in the host's glass for approval. After approval, serve similarly as in the service of white wine. Remember to fill the glass three-quarters full only.

- After serving place the bottle in the wine cradle. Place it on the table and display the label clearly. When the bottle is empty, check with the guest if another bottle is required, if yes, replenish with a fresh bottle of wine and serve in fresh glassware.

Service of sparkling wines

A bottle of sparkling wine is opened by first removing the wire cage and foil. Pointing the cork safely to a corner of the room, away from guests, grasp the cork firmly and twist the bottle to allow the internal pressure of the wine to push the cork out. Follow the same procedure for service as you would for a white wine.

Pouring of wine — Some important points

- Do not pour the wine from a height.

- Do not rest the neck of the bottle on the rim of the glass.

- Do not conceal the label of the bottle.

- Do not fill the glass to its brim. Fill only three-quarters full.

- Pour a little for the host to taste and wait for his approval. If the wine is approved, serve the lady seated to the right of the host first, and move clockwise serving all ladies around the table, followed by the gentlemen and finally the host.

- Twist the bottle over the glass after each serving, to prevent the dripping of wine from the rim of the bottle.

- Do not keep wine glasses empty for too long, as the temperature of the wine in the bottle may change and this may not be to the guest's liking.

- Put the bottle back in the wine chiller after service, with the label facing the guest. Be available to refill the glasses.

- When the bottle is empty, invert it in the wine chiller (only for white, rosé or sparkling wines) and check with the guest if a fresh bottle is required. If yes, replenish with a fresh bottle of wine and glassware.

Wine and food

There is no shortage of advice on what wine to drink with a particular dish. The most common belief is that one should drink white wine with white meat or fish, and red wine with red meat, but none of the conventions about pairing wine and food are rigid. In fact many varieties of wine — red, white and rosé do not necessarily have to follow this rule, but conventional patterns of matching wine and food provide guidelines to plan a successful meal with appropriate wines.

Food and wine should complement one another. A wine should complement the dish and enhance the dining experience.

However, there are some types of food that do not strike up a harmonious relationship with some wines and could spoil the meal if not matched correctly. Generally sharp flavours such as lemon or vinegar and wholesome ones such as chocolate clash with wine. Hence care should be taken during the planning and service of a meal.

A basic guide for matching French wines and food

Food	Wines
An apéritif	Champagne, Saumur, Vouvray
Shellfish	*Light bodied :* White Burgundy, White Bordeaux, Muscadet, Champagne, Alsace, White Bordeaux, White Burgundy, Vouvray, Beaujolais and White Vin de Pays.
Veal and Pasta Poultry and Salads	White Burgundy, Alsace, Red Bordeaux. Côtes-du-Rhône, Beaujolais, Anjou Rosé, White/Red Vins de Table and Vins de Pays.
Mild Cheese and Dessert	*Medium bodied :* Loire, Alsace, Beaujolais, Champagne, White Bordeaux and White Burgundy, Vouvray.
Beef, Lamb, Game and Robust Cheese	*Full bodied :* Beaujolais, Côtes du Rhône, Red Bordeaux, Beaujolais Crus, Côtes du Rhône, Red Burgundy and Red Bordeaux

SUMMARY

1. Wine is an alcoholic beverage obtained from the fermentation of the juice of freshly gathered grapes.

2. The Greeks introduced and spread the growing of the vine to Europe. The Romans continued to spread the making of wine through their provinces which provided wine for the entire Roman empire.

3. Grape vines can survive and produce fruit under the most extreme conditions. Adequate sunlight and a moderate winter are needed to produce grapes to make wine on a commercial basis.

4. Crushing, pressing, fermentation, racking, fining and maturation are different stages in the making of wine.

5. Wine may be classified into :

   a. Natural or still wine   c. Fortified wine

   b. Sparkling wine   d. Aromatized wine

6. Italy produces the largest quantity of wine in the world, while France produces the finest quality wines in the world.

7. Champagne is a region in France that produces the king of sparkling wines — *champagne*. It is produced by a special process that lays emphasis on secondary fermentation.

8. Italy, Germany, Portugal, Spain and Hungary are some of the other major wine producing countries.

9. California, Australia and South Africa also produce good quality wines that compare favourably with the best in the world.

10. Food and wine should complement each other. There should be harmony of food and wine during the meal experience.

Review Questions

Answer the following questions :

1. Define the word *wine* and describe the development of wine production.

2. Explain the expansion of the wine trade.

3. How is wine manufactured?

4. How are wines classified? Write a short note on each type.

5. Why should one have a knowledge of the various types of grapes used in wine making?

6. Identify some famous wine producing countries in the world.

7. Specify the categories of wines produced in France.

8. Outline the stages in the manufacture of champagne.

9. Give the rules to be observed for the correct service of wine.

10. Explain what is understood by harmony of food and wine.

11. What is the ideal temperature for the service of :
    i.   Sparkling wine
    ii. White and rosé wine
    iii. Red wine

12. Write a short note on :
    i.   Solera system
    ii. Appellation d'Origine Contrôllée

13. Name any five grape varieties used in making wines.

Projects

1. *Identify ten popular varieties of :*
   i.   *Still, red, white and rosé wines*
   ii. *Fortified wines and the spirit used for fortification*
   iii. *Sparkling wines and their styles*
   iv. *Aromatized wines and the flavours used*
2. *Make a table matching wines and food from different countries of the world.*

Glossary

Apéritif : An alcoholic beverage taken before a meal to stimulate the appetite.

Aromatized wines : Wines which have flavourings or botanicals added to them.

Bitters : An aromatic wine.

Bloom : A powdery substance found on the skin of grapes which is composed of tiny yeast cells.

Botanicals : Flavouring agents such as herbs, bark, roots, flowers or quinine.

Bouquet : The aroma normally associated with wine.

Carbonated : A liquid which has carbon-dioxide introduced into it to make it fizzy.

Dosage : Wine which is added to a bottle of champagne after degorgement. This determines the sweetness of the wine.

Fermentation : A chemical change that involves the conversion of sugar into alcohol.

Must : The product obtained when grapes are crushed. This is the first stage in the wine-making process.

Secondary fermentation : This takes place in sparkling wines, which is achieved by the presence of carbon-dioxide in the wine.

Sommelier : A person specially trained in the service of wines.

Vermouth : An aromatized wine flavoured with botanicals.

Vine : The plant which produces grapes.

Vintage wine : A fine wine produced from a harvest of grapes of excellent quality in a particular year.

Wire cage : A thin metal wire attached around the cork of a sparkling wine bottle to prevent the cork from popping out unexpectedly.

12

Cocktails and Non-alcoholic Beverages

Objectives : A study of this chapter would enable you to :

✧ *Explain what is meant by a cocktail.*

✧ *Understand the classification of non-alcoholic beverages.*

✧ *Differentiate between stimulating and refreshing or nourishing beverages.*

✧ *Discuss the varieties, the making and service of coffee and tea.*

Cocktails

A *cocktail* may be defined *as a delicate combination of ingredients with a spirit base, to which a single beverage or a variety of soft beverages with additives such as sauces, bitters and cordials are mixed.* All these give a cocktail its unique taste.

A *mocktail* is *a combination of two or more non-alcoholic beverages.* It is a non-alcoholic cocktail or a cocktail without the spirit base. Cocktails may be served as a short or a tall drink. They are normally served in special glasses with or without a garnish. However, garnishes make a cocktail appealing to the eye. Olives, cherries, pineapples, oranges, lemon and celery are used as garnishes.

For interest

The declaration of independence of the United States of America in 1776 coincides with the most plausible version of the birth of the cocktail. It is said that Betsy Flanagan, a barmaid in a tavern in New York State served a guest a mixed drink decorated with the tail feather of a rooster. The drink was dubbed a cocktail. The term is now commonly used in English language.

How to make a presentable cocktail

Cocktails can be shaken, stirred, blended or built. A *cocktail shaker* is used to mix ingredients that would not normally blend by stirring. It is made of either electro-plated nickel silver (e.p.n.s) or stainless steel.

A cocktail shaker consists of three parts — the *base to hold the ingredients,* the *strainer* and the *cover.* The *strainer* prevents the ice or any other ingredient from dropping into the glass when the cocktail is being poured. Shaking a cocktail is a very simple operation. The ingredients are placed in the lower half of the cocktail shaker with a few cubes of ice. They are shaken well, strained, garnished, if necessary, and served. Most of the cocktails are shaken, though some are stirred with a long glass or plastic stirrer or a swizzle stick.

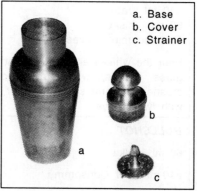

a. Base
b. Cover
c. Strainer

Fig. 12.1 *A cocktail shaker*

Cocktails can also be blended in a blender. Some cocktails are built carefully by pouring a light beverage on top of a heavier one making sure they do not mix, thus producing a cocktail with different layers.

Rules to make a perfect cocktail

- Use only the best known proprietary (trademark) brand of spirit.
- Make sure that the cocktail shaker is perfectly clean.
- Ice is used for nearly every cocktail recipe. Do not use the same ice again, though in a busy cocktail bar this may be unavoidable.
- The ingredients always mix better in a large shaker. Do not overfill the cocktail shaker.
- Shake the cocktail shaker vigorously for 15 to 20 seconds, using short snappy actions. Effervescent drinks should not be shaken.
- Chill the cocktail glass before serving.
- Serve immediately after shaking or mixing. Do not fill the glass to the brim.
- Always use the best quality olives, cherries and fresh or canned fruit as garnishes.
- When egg white or yolk is used as an ingredient, break the egg into separate bowls to separate the white and the yolk.

- Always place ice in the shaker or glass first, followed by non-alcoholic and then alcoholic beverages.
- As a general rule, stirred cocktails are based on liqueurs or wines (clear liquids).
- Ingredients used for shaken cocktails such as fruit juice, cream and sugar need a vigorous shake to blend properly.

Some cocktail recipes

MINT JULEP

A pinch of Sugar
240 ml Water
60 ml Whisky
Crushed mint leaves

Pour the whisky and water in an old fashioned glass. Garnish with dampened mint leaves, crushed ice and sprinkle sugar on top. Serve with two straws.

BULLSHOT

60 ml Vodka

240 ml Beef Consommé

Serve with ice cubes, garnished with a wedge of lime in an old fashioned glass.

TOM COLLINS

15 ml Sweetened Lime Juice
60 ml Gin
Soda

Shake well, pour the ingredients into a Collins glass filled with ice and top it up with soda. Serve garnished with a cherry and an orange slice.

AMERICANO

60 ml Dark Curacao
60 ml Brandy
15 ml Cream

Shake well and serve garnished with a twist of lemon and crushed ice in an old fashioned glass.

SINGAPORE SLING

60 ml Gin
30 ml Cherry Brandy
A dash of Lime Juice
Soda

Shake all the ingredients except soda with ice and pour in a highball glass. Top it with soda and garnish with an orange slice and a cherry.

CHAMPAGNE COCKTAIL

One cube Sugar
Two drops of Angostura Bitters

A glass of Champagne

Put a cube of sugar and angostura bitters in a glass and top it with champagne. Serve in a champagne saucer, garnished with a twist of lime.

Fig. 12.2 *Making a cocktail*

Fig. 12.3 *A cocktail*

Non-alcoholic beverages

These beverages are broadly classified as **hot stimulating** beverages and **cold refreshing** and **nourishing** beverages.

Hot beverages

Coffee and *tea* are hot beverages that are most often served in restaurants and hotels. Both coffee and tea can be made in different ways and are normally served from the pantry or any other appropriate service point.

Coffee

Coffee is made from roasted or unroasted *coffee beans*. Freshly ground coffee powder gives a very pleasant aroma, as the flavour and strength come from the oils in the coffee beans.

Storage of coffee

Coffee is an expensive commodity. Utmost care should be taken in its storage. Coffee beans/powder should be stored in an *airtight container* in a *well-ventilated room away from excess moisture* and *strong-smelling food,* as ground coffee tends to lose its flavour and aroma due to the evaporation of oils in the coffee powder.

How to make good coffee?

- Use freshly roasted and ground coffee.
- Match the correct variety of coffee to the type of machine used.
- Ensure that all the equipment used is clean.
- Use a set measure of coffee powder for each cup. Wrong measures can cause the flavour to fluctuate from cup to cup.
- Add boiling water to coffee and allow it to infuse. The infusion time should be controlled according to the type of coffee, the machine used and the method of making coffee.
- Control the temperature as coffee develops a bitter taste if allowed to boil.
- Strain and serve black or with milk or cream separately. Ideally coffee should be served within 30 minutes of being made. The most desirable temperature at which coffee should be served is 84°C.

What makes coffee taste bad?

- Not allowing the water to reach its boiling point or boiling it too long.
- Using coffee beans that are over roasted or not roasted properly.

- Using too much or too little coffee powder.
- Keeping infusion time too short or infusing it at a high temperature.
- Keeping prepared coffee for too long before service or serving reheated coffee.

Service of coffee

All food and beverage service personnel should know the various methods of serving coffee. The service of coffee is largely dependent on the method used to make it. Coffee should be served *piping hot,* at the *correct flavour* and *strength,* with the *right accompaniments* and in the *correct cups.*

Types of coffee

Filter or percolator coffee

The filter coffee machine has two parts — a *coffee pot* (at the bottom) and an *infusion pot* (on the top). After being infused through the coffee grounds, the filter coffee decoction is collected in the coffee pot. Since the coffee is placed on a hot plate, it remains hot and ready for service.

Cona coffee

This type of coffee is made and served from a specially designed glass case called the *Cona coffee machine.*

Turkish coffee

Finely ground coffee beans are used to make this type of coffee. The coffee powder is placed in a special copper jug and boiling water is poured into it and brought to boil. It is not filtered. A few drops of cold water are sprinkled on the top to help the coffee grains to settle. This should be done gently so as not to disturb the froth. It is then served in a demitassé. A drop of vanilla essence or a few rosé petals may be added to enhance its flavour.

Espresso coffee

This is Italian in origin. It is made in specially designed machines by passing steam through coffee grounds. Instructions for each machine may vary and they should be followed meticulously to achieve consistently high standards. The addition of milk or cream is optional.

Cappuccino

This is a strong black coffee similar to expresso coffee but with a chocolatey flavour. It is topped with cream or steam-frothed milk and sprinkled with chocolate powder.

Decaffeinated coffee

Coffee contains a stimulant called *caffeine*. When caffeine is removed from coffee it is called *decaffeinated coffee*. In Europe, it is referred to as *Café Hag* and in the USA, it is called *Sanka*.

Tea

According to a legend, about 5,000 years ago, a few tea leaves fell into a cup of hot water held by the Chinese emperor Shen Nung. The emperor declared the resulting brew a considerable improvement over plain water.

It was in the 17th century that the Dutch brought tea to Europe from China where it was grown in abundance. The British introduced it to India. Tea became the most popular beverage in a comparatively short period. Thereafter, the habit of drinking tea spread rapidly throughout the British Empire. Today tea is the most **widely consumed beverage.** It is estimated that one billion cups of tea are consumed everyday.

Tea is obtained from a tropical and subtropical evergreen shrub called *Camellia sinensis*. About 3,000 varieties of tea come from this plant and its many hybrids. After picking, the tea leaves are processed into one of the three basic forms of tea — *black, green* and *oolong*.

> ### For interest
> *The Boston tea party was a revolt by American colonists who refused to pay tax on tea. They threw crates of tea leaves into the sea in protest.*

Basic forms of tea

Black tea

The leaves are crushed and exposed to air to undergo chemical changes before they are dried. This turns the leaves brown and gives black tea its distinctive taste. More than three-quarters of the tea that is harvested in the world is made into black tea. This form of tea is consumed by most people in India, the USA and Europe.

Green tea

This is the oldest form of tea and is favoured by the Japanese and the Chinese. The leaves undergo less processing as they are only heated and dried to retain their green colour.

Oolong tea

This is a form of tea half way between black and green tea.

Storage of tea

Tea should be stored in *airtight containers* in a *moisture-free place* and *away from strong-smelling food*. The quantity of tea used per pot or per gallon may vary slightly with the type of tea used. Care should be taken while preparing tea in large quantities. It is normally brewed first and then served in large stainless steel *tea urns*. While brewing smaller amounts in the pantry, it is advisable to install a measure as a guide to be used so as to standardise and control the usage. Tea bags used these days serve as an in-built control measure and prevent wastage.

Making of tea

Warm the teapot with freshly drawn and boiled water. Add the correct amount of tea leaves — one teaspoon per person and one for the pot. Allow the tea leaves to steep in it for a few minutes. Using a tea strainer fill the teacup to a little more than two-thirds. Add milk if desired by the guest. Allow the guest to add sugar on his own.

Some points to be kept in mind while making tea

• Use good quality tea leaves.

• Use freshly drawn and boiled water. Over-boiled water makes tea insipid.

• Warm the pot with hot water before the tea is poured in it.

• Tea should be brewed and not stewed. The average time for the whole infusion process should be between 4 to 6 minutes. However, it may vary depending on the size of the teapot and the type of water used. The bigger the pot, the longer is the time needed for infusion. Soft water infuses more readily than hard water.

Service of tea

Place a small teacup, a teaspoon and a saucer in front of each guest. Place a small tray with a teapot, a hot water jug and a milk jug on the right-hand side for the guests to help themselves. Try to anticipate demands for extra hot water or milk. Some guests may like their tea black or with a wedge of lemon. Tea can also be served iced with a sprig of mint. The manner in which tea is taken is a matter of personal preference. It is advisable to check with guests as to how they prefer to have their tea served.

Cold beverages

Fresh fruit juice

This is the extract of juice obtained from fruits.

Natural mineral water

Natural mineral water is the water produced from natural water springs. It contains various minerals and in some cases, natural gases. The water comes from various parts of the world and its name is normally derived from its source or origin.

Natural mineral water is classified according to its most prominent physical and chemical properties.

Categories of Natural Mineral Water	
Apparent water	: *Arabella, Mount Mirabelle, Rubin*
Alkaline water	: *Evian, Air-les-bais, Chantilly, Vichy hospital, Vichy Celestine*
Ferrogenous water	: *Alberia, Spa, Vittal Homberg*
Sulphurous water	: *Aix-les-Chappal, Bonne*
Table water	: *Apollo, Burton, Malvel, Perrier*

Artificial mineral water

Artificial mineral waters are artificially impregnated with minerals and gases. Soda water, lemonade, tonic water, ginger-beer and ginger-ale are some examples.

Cordials and squashes

These are made from fruit juices and other flavours. They derive their names from the type of flavour used. They require diluting with water or soda. Some examples are lemon, cherry, strawberry, blackcurrant or pomegranate cordial, orange, mango or lemon squash.

SUMMARY

1. A cocktail is a delicate combination of beverages with a spirit base. It is served in a variety of glassware and has a unique taste of its own

2. A mocktail is a beverage that does not possess a spirit base. Only non-alcoholic beverages are used in a mocktail.

3. Non-alcoholic beverages could be classified as hot (stimulating) and cold (refreshing and nourishing) beverages.

4. Hot beverages comprise several varieties of coffee and tea.

5. Cold beverages include fresh fruit juice, natural mineral water, artificial mineral water and cordials and squashes.

Review Questions

Answer the following questions :

1. Define a cocktail. What is the difference between a stirred and a shaken cocktail?
2. List the instructions that should be followed while making a perfect cocktail.
3. Categorise cocktails based on the common spirit base, the glassware and the garnishes used.
4. Categorise the different types of coffee.
5. Explain what makes the coffee taste bad and bitter?
6. Describe the correct preparation and service of tea.
7. Explain the difference between artificial and natural mineral water.

Projects

1. *Gather as many plausible theories as you can, about the invention of cocktails.*
2. *Find out and list the most popular varieties of tea consumed in the world.*
3. *Identify the different brands of artificial and natural mineral waters available in your city.*

Glossary

Artificial mineral water : Water impregnated artificially with minerals and gases.

Cocktail : A mixture of alcoholic and non-alcoholic beverages.

Cocktail shaker : A container used for combining beverages by shaking vigorously.

Cordial : A fruit-flavoured drink.

Curacao : A liqueur of spirits flavoured with the peel of bitter oranges.

Decaffeinated coffee : Coffee which has no caffeine in it.

Demitassé : A small coffee cup.

Garnish : To decorate or embellish food or beverage to enhance its appearance.

Infusion : To steep in a hot liquid without boiling.

Mocktail : A mixture of non-alcoholic beverages.

Natural mineral water : Water produced from natural water springs and naturally impregnated with various minerals and sometimes gases.

Spirit base : A beverage that has a liquor base, for example, a cocktail.

Steep : To soak.

13

Tobacco
■■■■■■■■

Objectives : A study of this chapter would enable you to :
✦ *Identify the different varieties of tobacco and the countries where tobacco is grown.*
✦ *Explain the methods of curing tobacco.*
✦ *Distinguish between cigarette and pipe tobacco.*
✦ *List the sizes, strengths and brand names of different cigars.*
✦ *Understand and note the various points in the service of cigarettes and cigars.*

Tobacco

Tobacco is grown in countries with a tropical or semitropical climate such as Cuba, Jamaica, Sumatra, Philippines, India, Syria, Australia, Greece, Turkey, Egypt, Myanmar and parts of the USA.

The yellowish green leaves of the plant are harvested, dried and cured after which they are ready to be used by the cigarette or cigar manufacturer.

The two methods used for curing tobacco are :

• *Fermentative method*   • *Non-fermentative method*

Fermentative method

In this method, the curing is done by exposing the tobacco leaves to a temperature of about 77°C for 3 to 4 weeks. The leaves develop a distinct flavour and turn brown, glossy and pliable.

Non-fermentative method

In this process, the leaves are dried in the sun for about 4 to 5 days when the minimum temperature is between 18°C and 24°C and some moisture is also present in the air. The leaves turn light and yellow in colour. After curing in the sun, the leaves are subjected to a higher temperature for a particular length of time to retain the colour. To start with, they are subjected to a temperature of 37°C. This temperature is consistently raised to 82°C and is maintained for 4 to 8 hours. It is then decreased to 51°C, and retained for another 4 to 8 hours and is again slowly increased until it reaches 77°C. The tobacco is then considered *cured* and the leaves retain their yellow colour. *Chewing tobacco* is made by this sun-cured process.

Varieties of tobacco

There are four varieties of tobacco namely *brown, yellow, latakia* and *perique*. *Latakia* is a strong and dark variety, made from tobacco plants grown in countries such as Syria. This tobacco is cured by the fire of the Asiatic oak, which turns it into a dark colour. *Perique* is a similar variety and is grown in Louisiana. This variety is used to strengthen pipe tobacco.

Cigarette tobacco

The moisture and impurities present in the tobacco leaves are removed. The dried leaves are shredded by machines, rolled and allowed to mature. To make cigarettes, machines roll the tobacco in special tissue papers, gum the paper ends and cut the rolls into the required sizes. The cigarettes are then dried for 24 hours and mechanically packed. A comparatively small quantity of cigarettes are still made by hand for which a lot of practice and skill is needed.

Cigarette tips are of various types and these are called *filters*. *Cork tips* are most common in the West. *Filter tips* have a thin lining of cork obtained from the bark of the *querque tree* in Spain.

Pipe tobacco

The blending of the varieties of tobacco is normally done by experts. Correct proportions of strong tobacco such as *latakia* and *perique* are blended with lighter tobacco. Today's popular pipe tobacco combinations are composed almost entirely of *empire* tobacco, made from tobacco leaves from Zimbabwe.

Quality of cigarettes

Cigarettes made from *Virginian* tobacco are considered to be the best while Turkish cigarettes are the most aromatic and expensive in the world. Egyptian and Russian cigarettes are best appreciated after a meal or during the sorbet course due to the strong tobacco used in them.

Service of cigarettes

Cigarettes should always be served on a quarter plate with a doily paper as an underliner. The packet should be opened and several cigarettes should be partially pulled out of the packet. A box of matches should be placed beside the packet of cigarettes. A waiter should light the cigarette for the guest and extinguish the lit match by a swift downward swish of the hand.

The waiter should ensure that there is an **ashtray** on the table before cigarettes are served to a guest. Too many stubs should not be allowed to collect in the ashtray. The used ashtray should be replaced with a clean one. This is done by covering the used ashtray with a clean one and placing them on a salver, then replacing it with the clean one in the centre of the table.

Fig. 13.1 *Capping an ashtray*

Cigars

In earlier times, cigars used to be made by hand and were straight in shape. With the introduction of a wooden mould in which the leaves could be pressed into any desired form, cigar shapes were standardised. Cigars produced with the help of this mould came to be known as the **torpedor.**

> **For interest**
> *The cheroot, the Indian cigar, which has both ends cut, takes its name from the Tamil word 'shruttu' meaning a roll.*

The best quality of tobacco leaves for production of cigars are grown in Cuba, Java, Jamaica, Borneo and the East Indies. Tobacco of a lower quality is grown in India, Japan, South Africa, Holland, Russia and Hungary. The best cigars come from Havana in Cuba, though good quality cigars are also made in Jamaica, Mexico, Myanmar, India, Holland and Russia. Handmade cigars are preferred to machine-made ones.

The making of a cigar

A hard wooden board, a sharp knife to cut the wrapper, and scissors to trim the leaves are needed to make handmade cigars. Large leaves are selected for binding and several pieces of *filler* tobacco are arranged to make up the desired length, thickness and shape. The *filler* tobacco is rolled in a binder, then a wrapper leaf with the same characteristics is cut into the required shape and the whole lot is rolled. The vein of the outer leaf should run straight down the cigar. Moulded cigars are made in the same way, using moulds instead of being shaped by hand.

A cigar is composed of three parts — *Filler, Binder* and *Wrapper*.

Filler is the inner core of the cigar. It is made up of different blends of imperfect leaves of different varieties of tobacco that are broken up. The strength of the cigar depends on the filler.

Binder is made up of a single strong leaf to hold the filler together. The filler and the binder are together called *bunch*.

Wrapper is the outer wrapping of the cigar. It is made from the finest tobacco leaf. This makes it more presentable and aromatic. The outer wrapper is not necessarily obtained from the same source as the filler tobacco. In fact some cigars with Jamaican fillings have a Havana wrapper and these are indistinguishable in appearance and taste from the original Havana product.

Strength of cigars

The strength of a cigar depends on the filler and the wrapper as well as the curing and fermentation methods employed in making it.

Cigars are classified according to their sizes.

- Colorado Madurao (CM) : *Extra strong*   • Colorado (C) : *Strong*
- Colorado Claro (CC)   : *Medium*   • Claro (CCC) : *Mild*

Shapes of cigars

- *Bellied* or *torpedo* shaped in which both ends may be pierced or cut.
- *Round* or *flat* ended in which either end may be cut or pierced.

The colour of cigars ranges from light to dark brown, but this is no indication of their relative strength.

Quality of cigars

- A cigar should be smooth, firm and even to touch. The open or cut end should be evenly cut with a cigar cutter.
- A good quality cigar will produce a firm greyish ash which will hold for a long time before falling off.

Classification of cigars by size

A normal cigar or corona is 14.5 cm in length and 4.2 cm in band or girth.

Length of cigars		
La Senorita .... 10.5 cm	Corona Minor ... 14 cm	Petite Corona ..... 12.5 cm
Corona Major ... 13 cm	Royal Corona .... 14 cm	Grand Corona.... 14.5 cm
Hussar................ 15 cm	Lonsdale............ 16.5 cm	Monarch .... 18 cm

Service of cigars

- Cigars should be offered in cedarwood boxes.
- They should be stored in a humidor so that they do not lose their aroma and become dry or crumbly.
- A cigar cutter and a box of cigar smoker's matches which are longer and burn slower than the normal matches should be presented to the guest.
- The band of the cigar should be removed before smoking.
- If the cigar is not cut, a clean 'V' cut should be made from the rounded end with a cigar cutter to allow the smoke to be drawn easily through the *flue*.
- A cigar should not be pierced as it blocks the flow of air and the smoke gets a *tar* smell.
- A cigar should be lit by a match only, as fumes of the cigarette lighter may affect its taste.

Some popular brands of cigars		
Havana brands	:	*Romeo-y-Julieta, Bock-y-Cia, La Corona, Upman, Henry Clay, Bolivar, Cabana.*
Jamaican brands	:	*La Tropicana, La Invicita, Harry's Jamaica.*
Other brands	:	*Churchills, Pantellos, Margaritas, Lonsdales.*

Storing tobacco

- The ideal temperature for storing cigars and cigarettes is between 18°C and 32°C.
- A cedarwood case is preferred to any other kind of box, as its porous nature allows cigars to breathe.

SUMMARY
1. The two methods of curing tobacco are the fermentative method and non-fermentative method.
2. There are four varieties of tobacco — brown, yellow, latakia and perique.
3. Most varieties of cigarettes are made by machines that shred, roll and cut the tobacco into the required sizes.
4. Pipe tobacco consists of blends of strong and light tobacco.
5. A cigar consists of three parts namely the filler, the binder and the wrapper.
6. Cigars should be presented with a cigar cutter and a box of matches. They should not be lit with a cigarette lighter.

Review Questions

Answer the following questions :

1. Name the two methods of curing tobacco.

2. Discuss the varieties of tobacco.

3. Describe the non-fermentative method of curing tobacco.

4. Explain the ideal way to serve cigarettes.

5. List the various kinds of cigars.

6. How should cigars be served?

7. List the countries that are famous for producing good quality cigars.

8. How should tobacco be stored?

Projects

1. *Identify at least 50 popular brands of cigarettes from around the world.*

2. *Take a cross-section of a cigar and try to identify its different parts.*

Glossary

Cigar : It is made from tobacco leaves and is tubular in shape.

Cigar cutter : An implement used to cut the tip of a cigar before smoking.

Corona : A long cigar with straight edges.

Cure : To preserve by a special process.

Flue : The centre of a cigar through which smoke is drawn.

Humidor : A wooden box used for the storage of cigars and tobacco.

Querque tree : A tree grown in Spain whose bark is used to make the thin lining of cork found in the filter tips of cigarettes.

Virginian tobacco : Tobacco grown in the southern State of Virginia in the USA.

14

Safety and Sanitation in the Food and Beverage Service Department

∎∎∎∎∎∎∎∎∎∎∎∎∎∎∎∎∎∎∎∎∎∎∎∎∎∎∎∎∎∎∎∎∎∎∎∎∎∎

> **Objectives :** A study of this chapter would enable you to :
>
> ✧ *Understand the importance of safety at work.*
>
> ✧ *Identify the causes for breach of safety and the corrective measures to be taken.*
>
> ✧ *Highlight the steps to be taken to deal with a fire or a bomb threat at work.*
>
> ✧ *Understand how and why standards of sanitation should be adhered to.*

The importance of safety at work

All personnel should possess adequate knowledge of safety measures to be practiced while at work. Employees working in different outlets of the food and beverage department should be capable of using the service equipment in the correct manner. If instructions for the correct use of the equipment are not followed, it can cause injury to the user as well as damage the equipment. Training classes on safety at work are mandatory in most hotels. The food and beverage service department works under pressure, but still safety norms should not be overlooked.

Accidents can endanger both human life as well as the assets of the company. All personnel should be aware of the causes of accidents as well as the steps that should be taken to deal with them effectively. It is the responsibility of all employees to observe safety rules at work. This will prevent accidents and the consequent pain and loss of time.

Causes of accidents

Excessive haste : Excessive haste often leads to accidents. The golden rule is *do not run,* but this is difficult to observe especially during busy service schedules.

Distraction : Accidents are caused when one is not concentrating on the job at hand. *Lack of concentration* could be due to *loss of interest, carelessness* or *preoccupation with personal problems while at work.* Managers or supervisors should identify such problems of their personnel and give them a sympathetic hearing. They should check the reasons and take appropriate measures, such as counselling the employee or transferring him to a more suitable department or outlet.

Panic : A dangerous situation may crop up suddenly which could cause panic and lead to confusion. All service personnel should be adequately trained to handle such critical situations.

Some steps to follow during a crisis

* Do not waste time but immediately deal with the situation. This can prevent injury and loss of property.

* Report to the manager in writing about the situation. Most hotels have a policy for dealing with accidents. It should be strictly followed.

* Do not assume anything. Verify the problem before taking corrective action.

* Inform the concerned supervisor so that corrective measures can be taken to avoid such incidents in future.

* Contact authorities such as the police, fire brigade and ambulance, if need be, immediately.

Failure to apply safety rules : Safety precautions should be enforced in all operational outlets of the hotel. Service personnel should remember that rules are meant to be followed. Very often a daily routine in doing a particular task makes us careless and we resort to shortcuts. This is dangerous and should be avoided. All accidents should be reported to the manager at once.

How to prevent accidents?

The following precautions should be taken to avoid accidents :

* The floor should be kept clean and dry. Spilt food or liquid should be cleaned and wiped dry immediately.

* Equipment should not be left lying around but should be stacked in its correct place after use.

- Power cables should be checked properly. All electrical equipment such as hot plates should be serviced and cleaned regularly.
- Electrical circuits should not be overloaded.
- Heavy things should be carried properly. If the things are not carried properly they can cause injury to oneself as well as to one's colleagues.
- Keep sharp articles away from service areas.
- Store cutlery in racks or drawers with the handles facing the same direction.
- Clear up broken glass or china immediately, wrap it in a sheet of newspaper and place it in a bin.
- Hands and feet should be properly protected from heat, cold and cleaning agents. Cuts, grazes and wounds should be covered with a waterproof dressing.

Fire safety

How to prevent fire?

- Do not overload electrical circuits.
- All electrical equipment should be checked periodically. Faulty equipment should not be used.
- Ensure that an adequate number of ashtrays are available for guests. Always empty ashtrays into metal bins that do not contain paper or other inflammable material.
- Be careful while using a spirit or gas lamp on a guéridon. Put off the lamp if you have to move the trolley.
- Use fire resistant fittings and furnishings.
- Linen and spare furniture should be stored in a proper place.
- Keep passages and escape routes free from obstructions at all times.
- All alarm systems should be serviced by an approved contractor at least twice a year and details of the service, extent and faults should be recorded.
- Do not allow waste to accumulate on the floor. It should be disposed of properly.

How to deal with a fire at work?

A hotel can turn into a fire trap if the personnel are not careful or are not adequately trained to handle an outbreak of fire. Fires cause a huge loss of money and property, apart from causing injury or even death. Training classes are regularly held in all hotels to practice the evacuation of guests and staff in an orderly manner.

Steps to be taken when there is a fire

- *Raise the alarm :* Sound the alarm and inform the people in the vicinity of the fire. Also inform the manager on duty who will in turn inform the fire department.

- *Do not panic :* If you are trained in fire drill, offer assistance in a calm manner. If not, allow trained people to do so.

- *Use fire extinguishers :* If you are unsure of what to do, never put yourself at risk in attempting to fight a fire. In all areas of a hotel a variety of fire extinguishers are available to use on different types of fires. Familiarise yourself with the operation of these extinguishers and on what fires they should be used. Do not use the wrong extinguisher on a fire. It could make things worse.

Fire extinguishers and the fires they should be used for

Water extinguishers : They are used for fires involving wood, paper and cloth. They should not be used on live electrical equipment, burning fats or oils.

Carbon dioxide extinguishers : They are used for fires involving inflammable liquids such as oil, fat, petrol, paint and solid fuel. They can be safely used on live electrical equipment.

Foam extinguishers : They are used for fires involving wood and inflammable liquids. Instructions given on the extinguisher should be checked as some type of foam extinguishers are not suitable for live electrical equipment.

Powder extinguishers : They are used for electrical fires and fires involving inflammable liquids.

Fire blanket : This is used for fires involving burning liquids and clothing.

Steps for evacuation

Most hotels conduct practice fire drills as well as put up notices with instructions on how to fight a fire at strategic points for both guests and staff to follow. Ensure that you read and understand them and know what to do when the situation arises. If you cannot understand anything during a fire drill, inform the manager.

Some points to remember

- Sound the alarm.

- Instruct guests to head straight for a fire exit.

- Leave the building if possible, if not, assemble guests at a point to avail of assistance in the evacuation of the building.

- Do not run.

- Do not use lifts.

- Do not allow guests to go back for personal belongings.

- Do not open a door if you think there are flames on the other side.

- Do not allow guests to go back into the building until the *all clear* signal is given by the manager.

Bomb threats

In the event of receiving a bomb threat over the telephone, **record the message** in the exact words spoken by the caller. Note down the time the call began and ended. Attempt to get as much information as possible from the caller such as :

- The location of the bomb.

- What the bomb looks like?

- When and what will make it explode?

- The reasons for planting the bomb.

- Details about the caller that will help in identification —

  - Gender

  - Tone and type of accent used — was the voice calm, nervous, rambling, serious or drunk.

  - Were there any background noises?

You should then

- Cordon off the area under threat and calmly inform guests and staff to move away.

- Inform the manager on duty and the concerned authorities for further action.

- Allow people to return, only after the *all clear* signal has been given from a competent and recognised authority.

Sanitation

An excellent standard of sanitation has to be maintained in all outlets of the food and beverage service department. All food and service areas should be cleaned regularly. If not, there is every likelihood of attracting pests that can lead to diseases or cause food poisoning.

The following things should be done to keep the hotel and its surroundings clean and pleasant.

- The floor should be kept clean and dry at all times. The table tops should be kept spotlessly clean and dry.

- Furniture should be dusted and polished.

- Carpets should be properly vacuumed and shampooed, when necessary.

- All equipment in use should be well maintained and serviced regularly.

- A cleaning schedule should be planned and enforced. Most of the cleaning and maintenance of the premises and equipment should be done at night.

- Indoor plants should be watered regularly and replaced with fresh plants from the main garden at least once a week.

- The walls, floors and ceilings should be well maintained.

- Light fixtures, bulbs and switches should be checked regularly and faulty ones replaced immediately.

- Public area toilets should be cleaned regularly and checked frequently for soaps, towels and toilet paper.

- Dustbins should be kept covered at all times with tight-fitting lids. Uncovered bins in the kitchen attract flies and other insects. Fly-screens should be used to prevent flies from entering the areas where food is kept. Gadgets that kill flies should be mounted in the back area. A fly spray may also be used.

- Pesticides should be sprayed regularly to control pests. Special attention should be paid to the elimination of cockroaches in all areas.

- Rats, besides being destructive are carriers of diseases. Rat traps should be set at strategic places. Rat poison should not be used as it is difficult to keep track of dead rats. Frequent inspection helps to control these pests.

- Pest control firms which contract out their services to hotels and catering establishments should be contacted. They should regularly spray pesticides and set rat traps to free the establishment from pests.

SUMMARY

1. All service personnel should possess adequate knowledge of safety measures to be followed at work.

2. Accidents are caused by excessive haste, panic, distraction and failure to apply safety rules.

3. High levels of sanitation can be maintained, if regular cleaning and maintenance of property and equipment are practiced.

4. Controlling pests is an ongoing procedure and should be done regularly.

Review Questions

Answer the following questions :

1. Describe the importance of safety at work.

2. State the precautions to be taken to avoid accidents at work.

3. In the event of a fire in your work area, specify the correct procedure to be followed.

4. Describe the various fire extinguishers and the fires they are used for?

5. Describe how you would deal with a bomb threat.

6. Highlight the importance of sanitation in all food and beverage service areas.

Projects

1. *List the various kinds of accidents that may occur in the food and beverage service department, and the preventive measures to be taken for them.*

2. *Compare the standards of hygiene and sanitation practices in various food service outlets in your city and highlight steps that should be taken to improve them.*

Glossary

Carpet shampoo : A chemical used to clean carpets.

Evacuation : To remove people from a place of danger to stay elsewhere for the duration of the danger.

Fire extinguishers : Equipment designed specifically for putting out fires.

Fly-screen : A mesh that prevents the entry of flies.

Pesticide : A substance that is sprayed to kill insects.

Pests : Destructive animals or insects which attack food, crops and livestock.

Sanitation : The disposal of sewage and refuse.

Schedule : A plan of work or a list of intended events drawn up in advance.

15

Budgeting for the Food and Beverage Service Department

■■■■■■■■■■■■■■■■■■■■■■■■■■■■■■

Objectives : A study of this chapter would enable you to :

✦ *Understand the process of budgeting followed in the food and beverage department.*

✦ *Highlight the budgeting cycle and its objectives.*

✦ *Specify the qualitative objectives to be considered when planning a budget.*

✦ *Explain how a budget is prepared.*

✦ *State what is meant by food and beverage sales forecasting.*

Budgeting control

A budgeting control system that covers all the outlets in a food and beverage department is essential for the economic future of an establishment. Formulating and adhering to a budget, ensures the full utilisation of the potential of an establishment in attaining the desired revenue and profit margins.

Formulating a budget involves projecting or estimating future income, expense and profit over a fixed accounting period. Budgeting is regarded as an important management tool and is a critical instrument of planning and control. This can only be achieved if the policy of the establishment has been decided in advance. This policy should also bear relevance to the end result.

The rationale for formulating a food and beverage budget

- A food and beverage budget is a plan of action which shows what could be achieved, in terms of food and beverage sales, the sales mix, average spending power, cost ceilings and profit margins.

- A food and beverage budget helps in evaluating the current performance of an establishment. This can be done by comparing the actual sales and profit margins with the budgeted figures.

- A food and beverage budget helps to anticipate trends in the hotel industry and activities in a city. This enables the budget committee to identify slack periods and then decide how to utilise them during the forthcoming budgeted period.

- It enables the management to correctly anticipate, monitor and prepare for future business conditions.

- It gives the outlet managers involved in the preparation of the budget, an opportunity to establish their own operating objectives and evaluation techniques.

- It directs the management's ability to project estimates of future expense levels and may even serve as an instrument for setting proper menu prices.

In restaurants, independent of the rooms division, the food and beverage sales contribute upto 90 per cent or more of the total sales revenue. In hotels, the sale in food and beverage outlets is approximately 35 to 40 per cent of the total revenue. This indicates that the food and beverage operations of a hotel are of considerable economic importance and need detailed planning and strict controls.

An ideal formula for estimating budgeted profit is :

Forecasted income – Budgeted expense = Estimated profit

The Budgeting cycle

The budgeting cycle consists of six stages.

1. Formulating major objectives
2. Goal setting
3. Assessing prior period operating results
4. Analysing external environment
5. Performance and evaluation control
6. Budget preparation

Formulating major objectives

The major objectives should outline the profit margins the department aims to achieve during the forthcoming budgeted year. **Profit** is of prime importance in any food and beverage service outlet or restaurant. Hence while formulating a budget, an achievable profit target should be fixed. In the case of hotels, the profit target is expressed as a percentage of the entire unit's profit, whereas in an independent restaurant, the profit target is expressed as a percentage of the net profit, both in relation to the total turnover and the capital invested.

Goal setting

The management of a hotel should identify goals that are to be achieved by its food and beverage department for the forthcoming year.

In all food and beverage operations, the *sales volume* determines the *net profit*. A change in the sales volume has a direct effect on a large number of variables and controllable costs such as wages, power and food and beverage commodities. This directly affects the net profit of the department. Hence extreme caution should be exercised by predicting food and beverage sales separately.

Assessing prior period operating results

Profit margins and cost levels of the previous years of operation, are performance indicators which can be used as a yardstick for the current period. An analysis of the operating results in the past plays an important role in the preparation of the forthcoming budget in any food and beverage outlet.

The following factors should also be considered while assessing the prior period operating results.

- The number of covers (NOC) achieved for the entire operation, as well as for individual sales outlets.

- The average spending power (ASP) of guests in every section of the food and beverage department to establish the projected revenue of each outlet.

- In the case of a cocktail bar, the calculation of number of covers (NOC) and average spending power (ASP) is quite difficult, as an individual guest may frequently order drinks for several people. The budget could take into consideration the number of transactions that take place in the bar..This could be a much simpler and more effective method.

- The payroll is a major expense and has a tendency to rise regularly. Levels of wages, salaries and employee benefits for all departments should be ascertained. As a large part of a company's payroll is fixed, wages for part time and casual labour should be reflected in the fluctuations in the food and beverage sales volume. This is relevant to seasonal establishments as well as to those units which experience pronounced fluctuations in the sales volume.

- While most expenses tend to be fixed at least in the short term, several others are partially fixed and can be controlled through the budgetary process. Expenses such as gas, electricity, repairs and maintenance, laundry, cleaning, music and entertainment are called *operating expenses*.

All these objectives are expressed in quantitative terms, but the qualitative objectives that should be taken into consideration while planning a budget are also equally important. They are :

Quality of food and beverage : The standards set for the efficient functioning of a food and beverage outlet play a significant role in achieving the planned budget. The quality of food and beverages served should match the prices charged for them. The aspects normally taken into consideration are standardized recipes, present levels of skills in the kitchen, and the availability and condition of the service equipment.

Quality of service : This factor is very difficult to define and measure, but the effects of good or bad service become apparent by the increase or decrease in sales volume. Hence if service is inefficient, sluggish and unprofessional, provision should be made in the budget for remedial training of the staff.

Decor and ambience : This is an important aspect in the dining experience. Several establishments spend a considerable amount of time and money upgrading and maintaining the decor. The furnishings, carpets, wall coverings and colours used should be reviewed periodically and provision for change should be made in the budget.

Analysing external environment

Factors that constitute the external environment could include variables such as the economic climate of the country, corporate profits and the availability of disposable incomes. It could also include local trends such as the setting up or closing of industries in the vicinity of the establishment. It also depends on the establishment's ability to attract guests from all over the country and abroad to utilise the services offered.

Competition

- New or upgraded facilities of competitors should be monitored.
- Marketing techniques should be constantly reviewed and the strategies used by other establishments should be carefully studied.
- Menu prices for similar services offered in other establishments should also be considered.

Performance evaluation control

The food and beverage budget should be constantly evaluated. The evaluation consists of measuring the three major aspects that constitute a budget such as *income, expense* and *profit.*

Income : This refers to the income generated in all food and beverage outlets. The variance in income levels for each outlet should be evaluated regularly. An increase in the overall departmental income would point to a proportionate increase in variable expenses, though fixed expenses cannot be adjusted. An analysis of the income generated by the food and beverage service department guides the management in evaluating its strategies accordingly.

Expenses : Standards maintained in each outlet could be used as a yardstick by the management to determine departmental expenses. Expenses incurred may be either variable or fixed.

Variable expenses include gas, coal, electricity, water and raw materials.

Fixed expenses include staff salaries, uniforms, permits, equipment and maintenance.

If operational expenses are not monitored and controlled, it is difficult to generate the budgeted income, thereby affecting profit margins.

Profit : Budgets are formulated based on a given set of assumptions. If these assumptions change, so does the budget. Budgeted profit can be achieved, only if the food and beverage service operation provides adequate returns on risk and investment.

To meet budgeted profit margins, the monitoring of both income and expense is very essential to any operation.

$$Income - Expense = Profit$$

Budget preparation

The forecast of the budgeted sales volume, marks the beginning of the whole process of budgeting.

- The first step is to ascertain the revenue and expense figures of all the outlets for the current year. Figures of ten months can be considered for predicting the immediate future.

- The second step is to take into account the most recent trends and project the prospects for the following year.

- A decision has to be taken on appropriate percentage changes between the current year and the following year after considering all the relevant details.

- Finally, the current revenue and expense figures should be adjusted by appropriate percentages, thereby arriving at the sales figures to be achieved for the following budgeted year.

Limiting factors

There are several factors that prevent the proposed budgeted revenue and expense figures from being met. In each case positive steps should be taken to remove the negative influence of the limiting factors on the figures for the budgeted year.

Seating capacity : The revenue earned by an establishment could considerably improve if the *seating capacity is increased.*

Shortage of efficient labour : There would be a drop in clientele, if guests do not receive the kind of service they expect. To avoid this, *fresh recruitments* should be made periodically and *motivational training sessions* should be conducted for the existing staff.

Poor restaurant supervision : *Good supervision* improves guest satisfaction, thereby ensuring improved revenue and cost control for the outlet.

Insufficient capital : The organisation should have *sufficient capital* to *maintain*, *replace* or *buy equipment* when needed. The unserviceable equipment would eventually affect the service and thus prevent meeting the budgeted figures for the following year.

Annual budgets should be broken up into shorter periods such as weekly, monthly and quarterly estimates. This would enable the comparison of current performance against the budgeted target for a particular period. If there is a difference in the figures, the causes for the variance should be ascertained and evaluated. Remedial control measures should be instituted immediately to correct this variance in figures for the following budgeted period.

Food and beverage sales forecasting

Forecasting is the *process of establishing what will occur at a future point of time, or during a given future period.* It also means extending the existing trends into the future. While forecasting food and beverage sales, emphasis is laid on what determines the sales volume. The number of covers (NOC) and the average spending power (ASP) are forecasted separately for each outlet.

The sales volume is the product of the number of covers (NOC) and the average spending power (ASP) of each cover.

Trends in number of covers (NOC) are difficult to predict, while average spending power (ASP) to a certain extent can be predicted, though it is independent and influenced by various methods of merchandising. This should be borne in mind while converting forecasts into budgeted figures.

Budgeting for sales in a large hotel will be more effective and realistic if statistical data is reviewed properly. A review of the data of previous years will help in formulating the forthcoming budget more accurately, as well as in ascertaining trends in employment and disposable incomes.

However, in general a downward trend in employment and disposable incomes, will result in fewer meetings and conferences, as well as lower ASP figures for wedding receptions and similar functions.

Controls

This is a very important aspect of hotel operations. If a strong control system does not exist in an establishment, then the budgeting, planning and operational functions will bear no fruit.

An effective food and beverage control department will go a long way in boosting the revenue by saving costs, as well as in attaining the pre-set budgeted figures.

SUMMARY

1. A food and beverage budget is an estimate of the future income, expense and profit over a fixed accounting period. This guides the actions of the management in the food service industry.

2. The budgeting cycle consists of several stages, which should be taken into consideration while formulating a budget.

3. Factors that limit the attainment of budgeted figures are limited seating capacity, a shortage of efficient labour, poor supervision and insufficient capital.

4. There are several qualitative objectives to be considered when planning a budget. They are quality of food and beverage, service, decor and ambience and the competition.

5. Forecasting may be described as the process of predicting what will happen during a given period. This will help in planning the future budget for income and expenses in the food and beverage department.

Review Questions

Answer the following questions :

1. What do you understand by *food and beverage budget?*

2. Explain the rationale behind formulating a budget in the food and beverage department.

3. Describe the three most important stages in the budgeting cycle.

4. Describe the qualitative objectives that should be taken into consideration while planning a budget.

5. Explain the process of budget preparation.

6. Explain what is meant by food and beverage sales forecasting.

Projects

1. *You are a food and beverage service manager of a new hotel. How would you forecast the sales volume?*

2. *Conduct a research on the operating expenses that are likely to occur in a hotel with five food and beverage outlets.*

Glossary

Average spending power : The average capacity of a person to purchase goods and services.

Fluctuation : To change irregularly.

Forecast : To estimate or calculate beforehand.

Forward planning : To plan for the future.

Marketing strategies : Ideas used to promote a product or a service.

Planning : Organising how something should be done.

Remedial training : Training given to rectify errors.

Sales mix : Money received from selling a variety of items.

Sales volume : The total accumulated revenue from sales.

Variance : A discrepancy between statements or documents.

16

Communication in the Hospitality Industry

∎∎∎

> **Objectives :** A study of this chapter would enable you to :
> ✧ *Understand the definition and importance of effective communication.*
> ✧ *Identify the barriers and offer solutions in result-oriented communication.*
> ✧ *Describe the effective sending and receiving of messages.*
> ✧ *Understand the role listening plays in communication.*
> ✧ *List the ten commandments of effective communication.*

What is communication?

Communication can be defined *as the science and practice of transmitting information.* Effective communication depends upon the *accuracy, brevity* and *clarity* of what is being communicated.

Effective communication in the hotel industry

Almost all tasks in a hotel involve some form of communication. Effective communication leads to the smooth functioning of the hotel. If communication is improper or fails, then the operations get hampered with disastrous results.

Every act of communication has six elements :

i. The sender	iii. The message	v. The language
ii. The receiver	iv. The medium	vi. The context

Communication involves sending a message that may be verbal, written in words, in figures or diagrams or it may be in the form of gestures or facial expressions.

Types of communication

Communication in the hotel industry may be classified under four types :

Upward communication

This form of communication is transmitted from the junior members of the staff of a hotel to the senior members. At times, it may just be a routine task of passing on information about the reservation of a room or it may be to offer comments and suggestions to their superiors.

Downward communication

This type of communication involves passing information from a senior member to a junior member of staff. This could include a briefing to the staff or issuing instructions by the restaurant manager or reallocating duties to the service staff.

Horizontal communication

This kind of communication takes place among staff of equal rank during the performance of their jobs. For example, it may relate to a shift captain handing over duty to a reliever.

External communication

This communication is particularly relevant to the hotel industry as the staff constantly interact with guests and suppliers on a daily basis. Good communication on this front ensures smooth functioning and creates goodwill for the establishment.

Barriers to effective communication

Communication may not be effective due to several reasons. Understanding the reasons and correcting the imbalance helps the organisation to function smoothly. There are certain filters or barriers that prevent the messages from being transmitted effectively. These barriers are :

Lack of self-confidence

The communicator may not have the self-confidence to interact with others. The questions that are likely to cause concern to the communicator are :

- Am I capable of performing this act of communication?
- With whom should I share the information?
- Will I be understood? Will this affect my self esteem?

Attitudes about the message itself

- Is the information valuable?
- Did I perceive or understand the information correctly to be able to explain it to others?
- Is the information easy to transmit?

Sensing the receiver's reaction

- Has the receiver comprehended the message?
- Does the reaction of the receiver convey signs that the information has been understood?

Sending a message

Information may be transferred verbally or in writing. While attempting to communicate effectively, to an individual or a group, the following should be emphasised upon :

Verbal communication

Clarity of speech

The message should be brief, specific and to the point. The speaker should speak clearly with correct pronunciation. The correct usage of language without excessive use of technical jargon, makes the message easy to comprehend. It enables effective transference of information thereby ensuring accurate and effective verbal communication.

Feedback

The key to effective communication on the part of the speaker, is to obtain some form of feedback that the information has been properly received and understood by the receiver. If there is a communication gap between the speaker and the listener, the latter is liable to lose interest. Hence the speaker should initiate and receive feedback regarding the effectiveness of the communication.

To send a message effectively, two things should be done simultaneously :

- Use appropriate words to express what one wants to say.
- One should continuously look for signs of a positive nature from the listener to ascertain if the communicated message has been effectively understood.

Written communication

Inevitably, a lot of communication in a hotel will be in the form of letters, memos or reports. Written communication is often a valuable supplement to verbal communication. For effective written communication, the sentences should be short and the language should be easy to understand. The message should be clear and to the point.

Receiving a message

Three factors are important when receiving a message. They are :

- Listening effectively
- Comprehending properly
- Processing the information correctly

Sometimes the receiver may be preoccupied and may not gather the full impact of the message. The receiver may filter the message and the filtered message may not make any sense in its present context or the receiver may at times be insensitive to non-verbal communication. The sender's eyes, gestures and sometimes the overall posture, communicate messages that an insensitive listener may not receive.

Cultural differences such as accent and comprehension of language as well as environmental conditions like poor acoustics may also act as barriers between the sender and the receiver. An ideal listener should listen carefully and try to understand the frame of reference concerning the subject.

Towards more effective listening

Effective listening should be an *active process*. To make certain that the listener has understood what is being said, there should be some form of interaction on the part of the listener. One way to do this is to paraphrase or summarise what has been heard.

Highlighting non-verbal communication

There is a whole range of human actions and behaviour, other than the spoken word that have a communicative function. Non-verbal communication can replace or enhance speech and regulate the verbal communication process. The importance of the message can be emphasised by certain non-verbal cues such as facial expression, body movement and tone of voice. A listener should observe these non-verbal cues to have a better understanding of the message.

Grasping the main idea

An effective listener need not remember every word or fact that the speaker communicates, but the main thought or idea should be correctly heard. Listening effectively involves not just hearing the words of the speaker but grasping the main idea of the message.

Ten commandments for effective communication

A manager's prime responsibility is to get things done through the staff. An excellent idea or a well-reasoned decision can become ineffective if it is not transmitted properly to the concerned person. Communication, therefore is the most vital management tool. On the job, one communicates not only with words but also through actions and attitudes. The effectiveness of a manager depends upon how well he can communicate.

The ten commandments for effective communication are designed to enhance managerial efficiency by improving skills of communication with superiors, subordinates and associates.

Clarify the idea before communicating

The more systematically an idea or a problem is analysed, the clearer it becomes. This is the first step towards effective communication. Many acts of communication fail because of inadequate planning. Good planning should consider the goals to be achieved, as well as the attitude of those who will receive the communication and those who will be affected by it.

Examine the true purpose of each act of communication

Before communicating, one should be clear about what is to be accomplished with the message. It could be to obtain information, to initiate action or to change another person's attitude. Once the major goal has been identified, then the language, tone and total approach to serve that specific objective should be adopted.

Consider the total physical and human setting before communicating

Intent cannot be conveyed by words alone. Several factors influence the overall impact of a message that has to be communicated. One should be sensitive to the total setting in which one communicates. For example, the sense of timing is an important factor. The circumstances under which an announcement or a decision is made, the physical setting, the social setting which pervades work relationships within the company or department, the tone of the person who is conveying the message, custom and past practice, and the expectations of the audience should be borne in mind before making any communication.

Consult where appropriate, in planning an act of communication

While planning communication, or checking the facts on which it is based, it is often desirable or perhaps necessary to seek the participation of others. Such consultations often help to lend an additional dimension and objectivity to the message. Moreover, those who have helped to plan the communication, will give it their active support in its implementation.

While communicating, take care of the undertones, and the basic content of the message

Tone of the voice, expression and sensitivity to the responses of others, have a tremendous impact on those who receive the communication. When these factors are overlooked, communication often prompts an adverse reaction to the message, notwithstanding its basic content. Similarly, the choice of language predetermines to a large extent the response of the listener.

Convey something of value to the receiver

The communication is better received if it relates to the interests and immediate and long term needs of the receiver.

Follow-up communication

One's best efforts at communication may be wasted if there is no follow-up action to ascertain how well the message has been received. This can be done by asking questions, encouraging the receiver to express reactions, and periodically reviewing the performance resulting from the communication. Every important act of communication should receive feedback, for proper assessment.

Communicate for tomorrow as well as today

While communications may be aimed primarily at meeting the demands of an immediate situation, it should also be planned keeping the future needs in mind. All acts of communication should be consistent with the interests and goals of the establishment. It may not be easy to communicate frankly on matters such as poor performance or the shortcomings of a loyal subordinate, but postponing disagreeable communication makes things more difficult in the long run, and is unfair to the company as well as to one's subordinates.

Match your actions with your communication

In the final analysis, *the most persuasive kind of communication is not what one says but what one does. A supervisor's actions or attitudes should not contradict his words.*

Be a good listener

When we start talking, we often cease to listen or observe the other person's responses and reactions. At times we are guilty of *inattentiveness* when others are attempting to communicate to us. Listening is one of the most important, difficult and neglected skills in communication. We should *concentrate* not only on what a person is trying to convey, but also on its *implicit meaning, unspoken words* and *undertones.*

Communication between the service department and other departments

Effective communication between the personnel in the service department and the staff of other departments is very important. This is true especially between the service and production personnel. Service staff communicate regularly with the production personnel both verbally and in writing. Care should be taken while passing on verbal instructions given by guests. The service staff should be careful while writing the Kitchen Order Tickets. *Incorrect information, illegible handwriting or the use of inappropriate abbreviations* could lead to unpleasantness between the service and the production personnel.

A few progressive managements encourage personnel to air their problems at open meetings where each problem can be evaluated from the perspective of all concerned. This improves the service offered to guests and provides a healthy working environment.

SUMMARY

1. All tasks in the hotel industry involve effective communication and every act has six elements, namely the sender, the receiver, the message, the medium, the language and the context.

2. Communication involves sending a message that may be verbal, written or in the form of gestures or facial expressions.

3. Communication in the hotel industry may be classified as upward, downward, horizontal and external.

4. There are certain filters or barriers that prevent the message from being transmitted effectively. These should be overcome to ensure effective communication.

5. The act of result-oriented sending and receiving of messages requires clarity of expression and effective listening skills.

6. To complete the cycle of communication, an ideal listener should understand the expressed idea from the sender's point of view.

7. The ten commandments for good communication are designed to enhance efficiency by improving communication skills.

Review Questions

Answer the following questions :

1. Define communication.

2. State the main objectives of effective communication.

3. Name the barriers to communication and how does one overcome these barriers.

4. What should one observe when : *i. Sending a message ii. Receiving a message.*

5. Identify the various modes of communication.

6. List the six elements that every act of communication entails.

7. Specify the role listening plays in the cycle of communication.

Projects

1. *Imagine you are a manager in a hotel. Evaluate the methods of communication in your department and record ways of improving its functioning by outlining the improvements in the present system.*

2. *Make a report to demonstrate how important a role effective listening plays in the functioning of the food and beverage service department.*

Glossary

Communication cycle : All steps pertaining to an act of communication.

Feedback : Response or information about the result of an experiment/communication/process.

17

The Role of Related Departments in a Hotel

- -

> **Objectives :** A study of this chapter would enable you to :
>
> ✧ *Identify the different departments in a hotel.*
>
> ✧ *Understand the role of each department in a hotel.*
>
> ✧ *Highlight the functions of the various sections in the different departments of a hotel.*
>
> ✧ *Discuss the role played by the kitchen stewarding department.*
>
> ✧ *Explain the functions of the purchase department and the job responsibilities of the key personnel.*
>
> ✧ *Describe the functions of the control department and the relevance of food and beverage controls.*

The main operational departments

Most hotels are divided into separate departments to facilitate their efficient functioning. There are four main operational departments, besides several other non-operational and support departments. Every department contributes to the successful running of a hotel. Out of the four main operational departments, the food and beverage service department has already been discussed in detail. The other three departments are :

- Front office
- Housekeeping
- Food production

Front office

The front office is the first department a guest encounters on entering a hotel. It is therefore important to create a good impression with the front office, as most guests will judge the hotel by the reception and service they receive from the front office department. This department is headed by a *front office manager* who is responsible for its administration and operations. *Lobby managers,* who work in shifts round the clock, assist the front office manager. They effectively control the day-to-day activities of the entire front office department. They are to the front office what outlet managers are to the food and beverage service department.

The front office of a large hotel may be divided into various sections. These sections have their own staffing patterns for doing different tasks.

Some of the sections and staff of the front office are :

Section	Staff
Bell desk	*Bell boys and bell captains*
Reception	*Receptionists and counter assistants*
Cash	*Cashiers and night auditors*
Reservations	*Reservation supervisor and clerks*
Portico	*Doormen, parking attendants and drivers*
Telephones	*Operators*

In addition to these, there are *airport representatives* who solicit business from arriving air passengers. They report to the front office manager or the *sales manager* depending on the policy of the management. The front office department works closely with the other operational departments, especially housekeeping.

When a guest enters or leaves the hotel, it is the front office which handles the check-in and check-out. Each personnel in this department plays an active role in the smooth functioning of the department to ensure maximum guest satisfaction.

Housekeeping

This department works in close coordination with the front office. It is primarily responsible for the cleaning of the rooms and public areas, maintaining the laundry, gardens and supplying flowers to all the departments of the hotel. An *executive housekeeper* runs the department with the help of the *supervisory staff.* This department is also divided into several sections.

Some of the sections and staff of the housekeeping department are :

Section	Staff
Housekeeping supervisor's desk	*Desk supervisor*
Floor and public area staff	*Supervisors, maids and housemen*
Linen room	*Linen room attendant*
Laundry	*Laundry men*

All these personnel perform their assigned duties independently and are responsible for the smooth functioning of the housekeeping department.

Food production

This department works in close association with the food and beverage service department. It is responsible for the preparation of food served in all the outlets of the hotel. The department is divided into different sections and each section is responsible for a specific type of cuisine or preparation. This system is prevalent in India, and is based on the *French kitchen brigade system* with some changes to suit Indian conditions.

The kitchen is divided into :

i.   Continental
ii. North Indian and *tandoor*
iii. South Indian
iv. Chinese
v.   Pantry
vi. Garde Mangerie
vii. Bakery
viii. Butchery

This department is headed by an *executive chef* who is responsible for both the administrative and operational aspects of the kitchen. The chef is assisted by one or more *sous chefs*. A *chef de partiè*, works under the guidance of the *sous chefs*, and is in charge of the section. The *commis* and the *trainees* report to the *chef de partiè*. Together they ensure that the food produced is of a high standard, and the operations of the food production department go on smoothly.

Non-revenue or support departments

A hotel cannot function with the main operational departments alone. Several other support departments are needed to make it fully functional. The various support departments are :

- Personnel
- Security
- Maintenance and Engineering
- Sales and Marketing
- Accounts and Administration
- Stores and Purchase

The staff of these departments work together under the leadership of the *general manager*, who guides them and coordinates the functioning of all departments, so as to make the hotel an attractive place for guests and a profitable venture for the management.

Kitchen stewarding

This department plays an important role in the functioning of both the food production and the food and beverage service departments. It is headed by a *chief kitchen steward* who reports to the food and beverage manager. Several *shift supervisors* work under the chief kitchen steward and each of them is responsible for carrying out the assigned tasks. Each supervisor in turn has *a team of utility workers* who do the manual work of the department. They are mostly unskilled workers who have to be trained and supervised effectively to ensure that they do the jobs assigned to them properly. This is a 24-hour department and is one of the mainstays of the food and beverage department.

Though the operations of the kitchen stewarding department are mainly in the back area, it is still one of the most important departments. Strict vigilance can control wastage and keep costs down by monitoring breakage, controlling supply of gas and coal to the kitchen and liaisoning with the maintenance department for preventive maintenance, and getting equipment repaired when necessary.

The job responsibilities of the personnel in this department include :

- Polishing all electroplated nickel silver (e.p.n.s) and stainless steel equipment.
- Maintaining cleanliness in the kitchen, back areas, staff cafeteria and of the kitchen equipment.
- Monitoring the garbage disposal system — collecting and periodical clearing of wet and dry garbage as well as emptying bottles and tins.
- Cleaning staff lockers. *(This job is sometimes done by the housekeeping department)*
- Cleaning the receiving area.
- Monitoring the supply of gas and coal to the kitchen and maintaining the gas bank.
- In some establishments, this department also looks after the meal service in the staff cafeteria.
- Taking periodic inventories of all kitchen and restaurant equipment. Keeping track of breakage and necessary replacements after informing the departmental head.
- Dish and pot washing.

Equipment used in the kitchen stewarding department

In all large hotels, a dishwashing machine has become indispensable to the kitchen stewarding department. The one most commonly used is the *spray type machine*. If used properly it can save a lot of time and effort and reduce the number of staff required for dishwashing.

Dishwashing machine

The spray type of dishwashing machine performs two basic functions :

- It washes and removes the stains from the dishes using a solution of detergent.

- It then rinses off the solution.

How does a dishwashing machine work?

The machine transports the dirty dishes on a conveyor belt to the *pre-wash chamber*, where a spray of hot water is pumped in to remove most of the food debris. The greasy food which floats to the top of the tank is removed through an overflow pipe. When the dishes on the conveyor belt reach the *wash stage*, the process is repeated using a detergent. The detergent completely removes all the stains. The dishes are now conveyed to the *pre-rinse stage* where sprays of hot water remove most of the detergent. In the final rinse, the remaining detergent is removed. Hot water used at this stage acts as a *sanitizer*, killing bacteria. A rinse additive is injected into the final rinse water to provide a *sheeting* effect for quick drying of all the washed dishes and to prevent water stains. The plastic curtains in the machine prevent splashing of water from one stage to another. Using a dishwashing machine is both hygienic and economical.

Purchase department

Purchasing may be defined as *the performance associated with the search, selection, purchase and storage of commodities, according to the requirements of the establishment.* Hence the purchase department is not only responsible for the purchase of different equipment and commodities but also for the performance of all tasks before the actual purchase of goods upto their usage by the user departments. An efficient purchase department with an effective and practical operating system will help in controlling the cost of materials and thus lead to significant savings. By making its operations cost effective, the establishment can attract more clients.

The purchase department is headed by a *purchase manager* who ensures the efficient functioning of the department by instituting practices that are both practical and systematic. The purchase manager oversees all activities pertaining to the purchase department and the receiving area.

The purchase manager's main duties include :

- Selecting cost effective goods, without compromising quality.

- Ensuring an uninterrupted supply of necessary commodities.

- Sourcing new products in the market, ensuring the availability of products and constantly monitoring prices.

- Purchasing commodities on a regular basis and responding to requisitions from user departments.

- Monitoring the standards and supply of commodities used by the hotel and preventing unnecessary stockpiling by different departments.

- Assessing the future price trends based on past records, reducing the expenses on purchases for all departments in the hotel, so as to establish a greater profit margin without sacrificing quality or obstructing regular supply.

- Maintaining regular contact with heads of different departments, and informing them of the availability of new products in the market for their use.

- Liaisoning with other departments such as accounts, controls and stores.

- Keeping senior management informed of the developments and changes, if any, that may adversely affect the performance of the purchase department such as variances in market prices.

If a hotel has an efficient purchase department, it will save a great deal of money and make the day-to-day functioning of each department more profitable by ensuring a regular supply of materials. The purchase department should maintain specifications for various commodities and the quality, standards and amount of use of all material by the various departments of the hotel.

How does the purchase department work?

Purchases made by this department are dependent on two factors —

- Regular purchases are made on the advice of the storekeeper who maintains a par stock of all the items that are regularly used in the various outlets of the hotel.

- Purchase of certain commodities is also made based on an authorised purchase indent.

Hotels have regular suppliers selected on the basis of tenders offered by them for the supply of specified goods that are in constant use. They supply goods for a fixed period of time at a predetermined price. This assures the hotel of a constant supply of goods throughout the year at a reasonable price.

Receiving area

This area of the purchase department also plays an important role in the whole chain of activities. If one does not have an experienced and technically sound *receiving staff,* then this area becomes a weak link, in the whole process of purchasing and issuing.

The staff working in the receiving area have to perform the following tasks :

- Check that the supplier delivers exactly as ordered, at the proper time and at the correct price.

- Weigh and measure all goods received, check against purchase indent, enter the details in the *goods received note* and dispatch the goods to either the stores, or to user departments, depending on the policy of the management.

- It is advisable to have a representative of the user department to check that the goods received match with the specifications of the needs of the department. Constant monitoring of this area is essential. If this area is neglected, then irregularities may take place and this could be detrimental to the profits of the hotel.

Stores department

The stores department keeps a stock of necessary commodities at all times, and ensures their regular and timely supply for the immediate needs of the establishment. Perishable items that are received by the receiving clerk, are normally issued directly to the kitchen while non-perishable items are sent to the stores, where they are stored item-wise and issued according to the policy of the establishment. The successful functioning of a hotel depends upon the timely availability of raw materials and other articles required by its various departments. Therefore, the *storekeeper* who handles this responsibility should be an efficient person with a systematic approach. He should arrange the items in such a manner that issuing, stacking and inventory taking becomes as simple and practical as possible. For example, regular items to be issued on a daily basis should be kept near at hand to facilitate easy accessibility and distribution.

When goods are received from the receiving department along with the *goods received note,* the storekeeper should cross-check the items received along with the goods received note, and store these items in their correct storage area. He should then enter in the records the names of the items received. No item should enter or leave the stores without proper documentation. He should issue items only on receipt of a *stores requisition form* duly authorised by a manager of the department. In most hotels the storekeeper makes a schedule for issue of items to different departments. This enables him to plan his daily work in a systematic way. If certain items are received in the stores, that the user departments are unaware of, it is the storekeeper's duty to keep them informed.

Regular inventories should be taken to constantly monitor the stock. In large and busy hotels there may be a separate *general store*, as well as a *food* and a *liquor store*. This helps to ease the pressure of daily issues from one place.

The stores department works under great pressure. Receiving a large number of items, both perishable and non-perishable, to cater to the needs of the various departments of the hotel and issuing them in response to their requisitions is a huge task. In case of an emergency, requisitions are also received during the night. Further, these activities have to be accompanied by maintenance of meticulous records, containing relevant details about the receipts and issues. These operations can be carried out only by a highly efficient storekeeper. The storekeeper is also expected to make sure that there is no understocking or overstocking of goods, since the former can cause inconvenience to the departments concerned while the latter amounts to unnecessarily tying up funds. Due to the use of computers, the functioning of this department has undergone a drastic change. It has made it easier to keep track of items, monitor re-order levels, stock control and to maintain proper inventories.

Food and beverage control

The food and beverage control department functions in close coordination with both the *chef* and the *food and beverage manager*. This department is headed by a *controller* whose main job is to monitor and control the costs of food and beverage. Monitoring costs of food and beverage is a continuous process. It helps the establishment to make necessary adjustments in its procedures and revise the prices of its food and beverage services as and when necessary.

The main tasks of the food and beverage control department are to :

- Ensure that everything issued from the kitchen and bar areas is accounted for.
- Ensure that all food and beverage items ordered by guests are charged for.
- Ensure that the correct payment is received for goods and services.
- Work out costs for food and beverages.
- Monitor yield analysis.
- Maintain checks on inventories.
- Control all requisitions and indents.
- Control ingredients by standardising recipes.
- Monitor and match Kitchen Order Tickets with bills.
- Check revenue against costs and prepare discrepancy reports.
- Minimise wastage and pilferage.

Kitchen Order Ticket (K.O.T) control

A variety of control systems are used in the hotel industry. One such important control system is the *K.O.T control*. When an order is taken from a guest, it is recorded in triplicate on a *Kitchen Order Ticket*. One copy goes to the kitchen, against which the *chef* prepares the dishes ordered for. The second copy goes to the cashier to make the bill. The third copy is the waiter's copy, against which the food or beverage to be served to the guest is picked up.

Subsequently, the controller receives and compares these copies to ascertain that there are no discrepancies. If he finds any, a discrepancy report is filed with the food and beverage manager for remedial action. This procedure is followed for all the outlets to exercise proper control over all food and beverage operations.

SUMMARY

1. The four main operational departments in a hotel are front office, housekeeping, food production and food and beverage service.

2. The front office and housekeeping departments work in coordination to see that guests are received, rooms are cleaned and let out to guests.

3. The food production department is responsible for the preparation of food to be served to guests in all the outlets of a hotel.

4. The kitchen stewarding department plays an important role by maintaining hygiene in the kitchen as well as taking inventories of all food and beverage equipment.

5. The purchase department is responsible for the purchase of different equipment and commodities required by the various departments of a hotel. This department works in close coordination with the stores.

6. The food and beverage control department's main task is to monitor and control the cost of food and beverages.

Review Questions

Answer the following questions :

1. Identify the main operational departments in a hotel and state their functions.

2. List the support departments in a hotel. Why are they called support departments?

3. Highlight the job responsibilities of a chief kitchen steward.

4. Describe the role of a purchase manager in a hotel. How does a well organised purchase department function?

5. Why is there a need for a control department in a hotel?

6. Outline the job responsibilities of a storekeeper.

Projects

1. *Identify the support departments in a hotel and list the job specifications of the personnel in each department.*

2. *Imagine yourself to be the food and beverage controller. Make a report on your job responsibilities.*

3. *Imagine you are the purchase manager of a large hotel. Highlight your role in making the hotel profitable.*

Glossary

Airport representative : An employee of a hotel, based at the arrival lounge of an airport, who solicits business for the hotel.

Check in : A guest arriving and registering at the front office of a hotel.

Check out : A guest leaving the hotel after clearing his dues.

French kitchen brigade : Kitchen teams based on the French system.

Gas bank : A place where all the gas cylinders are kept, and from where the gas is piped into the kitchen.

Non-revenue departments : Departments in a hotel that do not earn any revenue directly, but support the revenue generating departments.

Receiving area : An area where suppliers deliver, and the hotel receives goods for use by all the departments.

Sheeting effect : An effect produced in a dishwashing machine that prevents the formation of water stains on the articles and aids their quick drying.

Sourcing : To find out the terms and conditions under which items are available (cost, quantity, stock position etc).

Tender : An offer to supply a certain item at a fixed price for a specified period.

Yield analysis : A study of how much a food product will produce for final use. For example, yield from meat after removing bones and cooking.

18

Career Prospects in the Food and Beverage Department

■ ■

> **Objectives :** A study of this chapter would enable you to :
>
> ❖ *Explain the phenomenal growth and development of the hotel industry, and the opportunities open to prospective hoteliers.*
>
> ❖ *Guide students intending to study a course of hotel management.*
>
> ❖ *Explain the various career options available in the hotel industry.*
>
> ❖ *Describe what career options one can expect on the successful completion of a hotel management course.*
>
> ❖ *Explain the use of computers in the food and beverage service department, and the importance of knowing how to use them effectively.*

Growth

The hotel and tourism industry is one of the fastest growing industries in India. The hotel industry is a service oriented industry run by the people and for the people. With the advent of modern technology the industry is poised for further growth. An unprecedented growth in the economy has changed the lifestyle of a large cross-section of society. Today, people all over the world travel more frequently both for business and pleasure. There is also a growing awareness among people that a vacation away from home can be a positive and welcome change. A few years ago, most people did not take a planned vacation, and if they did, they travelled between their own home and a relative's home for a break. Nowadays many people visit places where they do not have any relatives, thus using hotel accommodation, and availing of the services provided by the hotel and tourism industry.

The demand for hotel rooms to accommodate all these people on the move is on the increase. A number of hotels/restaurants all over the country have sprung up to cater to their needs. When people travel away from their homes, they need other services such as food, entertainment, business and leisure-linked activities. To provide these services to discerning travellers and guests, the industry provides not just a room and a restaurant, but a specialised experience created by professionals. The Government of India and the individual State Governments have approved the addition of numerous hotels, resorts and restaurants to the already existing numbers.

Star rating

There is a grading system for hotels and restaurants, governed by the tourism department. This is generally referred to as the *star rating system*. This enables a guest to select a hotel based on one's needs and match the budget to the grade of the hotel one wishes to patronise. Modest hotels on the lower scale of the price index are normally the **one star** hotels that provide the basic amenities with no frills attached for a nominal charge. The deluxe and more elegant hotels are at the top of the rung, and they are categorised as **five star deluxe** hotels. Each star should satisfy certain criteria. For example, a five star hotel should have rooms that are of a particular size, with individual baths of an excellent standard, several restaurants, a 24 hour room service and coffee shop, a bar, banquet and convention facilities, a shopping arcade, a health club and swimming pool, a beauty parlour, channel music and cable television, in addition to a travel desk to provide travel related services. The food and service without doubt should be of the highest standards.

Global industry

Hotels are either single owner properties or a chain of hotels under one company name. There are international chains operating in India, as well as Indian chains operating abroad. Indian hotels operating abroad are reputed to be among the best in the world. Many three and five star hotel chains of international repute are slowly finding their way to India and the hotel industry is fast becoming a *global industry*. There are hotels to suit every budget, from small independent *budget hotels* to the more affluent and luxurious *upmarket hotels,* from *business hotels* to *leisure resorts,* from *casino hotels* to *floating hotels* at sea. Apart from these, there are restaurants that are independent of hotels. They are bars, pubs, fast food restaurants, contract caterers, industrial caterers, hospital caterers, function caterers, convention centres and various other food related services.

The world has never before seen such a *phenomenal growth in the food and beverage business,* and we in India are experiencing a similar trend. A few years ago the varieties of cuisines and styles of restaurants that were available in India were limited, but today urban Indians are more adventurous in their eating habits. They are no longer content with just *paneer tikka* and *murgh makhni,* but also relish *tacos, nachos* and *dim sum* among other specialities of the world. It is much easier these days to experience and taste the food of other lands due to the inflow of many foreign tourists. The numerous international companies setting up shop in India and the demand created by the internationalisation of the food industry have also contributed to the setting up of new food specialities. The major players in the hotel industry hold regular *food festivals* of international food as well as food from other States of the country. Foreign food festivals bring in chefs of international repute who cook their chosen specialities, using authentic ingredients that provide a taste of their country's cooking.

Indian chefs attend Indian food festivals abroad and participate in *culinary skill competitions.* This creates an awareness about the hotel and food industry, as well as about the people who provide these services to the paying customer. The variety of restaurants, pubs and international fast food outlets that have opened their doors for business, clearly indicate the existence of a growing demand for these services, and this trend is a pointer to the future as far as the food and beverage industry goes.

Prospects in the hotel industry

Career opportunities in the hotel industry are open for both boys and girls.

Apprenticeship

One can join the hotel industry as a **trainee** or **apprentice** at the staff level, and avail of the hotel's in-house training program while putting in a full day's work. The minimum qualification is a pass in Class X and the ability to communicate fluently in English. The candidate should be smart, pleasing by nature and possess a willingness to learn. The hotel ambience inculcates in one a dignity of labour. Most jobs at this level involve a hands-on approach. *Growth depends on how fast one learns, how well the assigned tasks are performed and how well one is able to work in a team.* The food and beverage service department involves all members of the team working in an atmosphere of professional and productive camaraderie.

Management trainee

As a graduate of any discipline, one can gain entry into the hotel industry as a **management trainee.** The entry level is that of a **supervisor,** which will eventually lead to career opportunities at the junior management level, in any of the hotel's departments.

Aspirants to a career in hotels, could also take a course in **Hotel Management** as this gives a clear indication of one's intention of pursuing a career in the hotel and catering industry.

If one enters the food and beverage service department directly, without any formal training in hotel management, one has to start at the lowest rung of the hierarchy as a **trainee waiter** or **trainee cook.** Promotions are based on the ability to work hard and effectively perform day-to-day duties. The road to achievement usually takes a little longer under these circumstances.

If one pursues a course such as a *diploma* or a *degree* in hotel management, one could gain entry at the **supervisory** or **junior management level.**

Career in a hotel and working conditions

Most hotels provide *pleasant working conditions* which in itself is a good motivator. There exists a shortage of trained manpower in hotels today, both in India and overseas. Hence efficient and productive hotel employees are always in demand. Salaries are generally good. The perks include in some places subsidised or free food on duty, company accommodation and most of all the opportunity to meet interesting people. The hotel industry also trains its employees to communicate effectively, to become self confident, develop good inter-personal relations, be well informed and to become highly successful organisers.

Training

The process of economic liberalisation and structural adjustment, has now entered a new phase of maturity. As an outcome of this process, there has been an upsurge in the demand for trained managerial cadres. With the continuing liberalisation and globalisation of the economy, demand for these cadres is expected to remain high, not only in terms of numbers, but also in terms of greater qualitative skills. To keep pace with the intensely growing competition, specialisation has become more than a necessity, and this realisation has paved the way for a phenomenal growth of Hotel Management schools in the country. This growth is expected to cater to the growing number of management cadres required by the industry.

Courses offered by Institutes of Hotel Management

The Union Government's Department of Tourism, has set up a National Council for Hotel Management and Catering Technology (NCHMCT) at Pusa, New Delhi. NCHMCT conducts a joint entrance examination to the three-year Diploma

Programme in Hotel Management and Catering Technology at 19 Government sponsored Institutes of Hotel Management. A three-year bachelor's degree course in Hotel Management is offered by several universities in India. The degree and diploma course in Hotel Management is the recognised entry level in the industry for a supervisory or management trainee's position. These multi-disciplinary courses prepare students not only for a job, but for a new way of life. They develop etiquette and manners which are so vital in the hotel industry. Skills which are absolutely necessary for a managerial position in the hotel industry also form a part of these courses.

Some subjects taught during the course include theory and practicals in —

- Food and Beverage Service
- Housekeeping
- Food Production
- Front Office

Theory subjects include —

- Financial Management and Principles of Management
- Sales and Marketing
- Economics and Hotel Laws
- Maintenance and Engineering
- French

Along with these, many other subjects are also taught. Each operational subject includes practical training on the job, during which a student will be taught specific practical skills to be able to face the challenges to be eventually met in the hotel industry.

The hotel industry is a hands-on industry, hence a lot of emphasis is placed on the practical aspect of the course. Most colleges stress on vocational training in the hotel industry during the course, so that students may learn through experience in the actual working environment. This is very important and makes the transition from a student to a full time employee much easier. This also helps a student to decide which department he would like to work in and also gives the management a chance to observe students at work and earmark them for absorption after their course.

Some chain hotels in India :

- Indian Tourism Development Corporation
- The Oberoi
- The Taj Group of Hotels
- Welcome Group
- Holiday Inn
- Quality Inn
- Ramada Inn
- Hyatt Regency
- Le Meridien
- Ramanashree

Use of computers in the food and beverage service department

Information technology assumes great importance in the era of globalisation of the hotel industry. It has changed the old operating systems and practices related to the hotel industry. The use of computers in the hotel industry has been steadily growing.

Computers are a valuable management tool, as they are used to collect, store and provide information in a systematic manner whenever needed. This information can be reproduced systematically in any format for further analysis. The increased use of information technology is a change from recording and communicating information on paper to digital electronic recording via computers.

Computers are being used in the hotel industry for —

- Inventories and stock taking
- Catering controls
- Sales point records
- Generating reports

- Budgeting in all departments
- Kitchen production controls
- Record keeping
- Financial analysis

Today, many software packages for hotels are available. These make the most arduous and time consuming tasks simpler. It is advisable to have a working knowledge of computers and many hotel management courses have included some form of computer study in their curriculum.

SUMMARY

1. With growing liberalisation, there is a great need for skilled professionals in the hotel industry.

2. Career opportunities are open for both girls and boys in the hotel industry.

3. Since the hotel industry is a hands-on industry, a lot of emphasis is laid on the practical training of professionals.

4. Several international hotel chains operate in India, giving ample scope for job opportunities in the industry.

5. Knowledge of computers is important for the hotel industry.

Review Questions

Answer the following questions :

1. Explain why the hotel industry is considered to be one of the fastest growing sectors in India.

2. List the courses offered for those who want to work in the hotel industry.

3. Name some international hotel chains that have units in India.

4. Describe the use of computers in the food and beverage service department.

5. Write a short note on the star grading system of hotels.

Projects

1. *Identify three to four popular hotel establishments in the city. List their attributes and grade them suitably as star hotels.*

2. *Prepare a brief note highlighting the job opportunities in the hotel industry.*

Glossary

Apprentice : A person learning a trade by being employed for an agreed period of time at low wages.

Casino hotels : Hotels which provide guests the facility of playing games of chance.

Food festival : A special occasion where the food and culture from a specified area of the world is presented to guests.

Star rating system : A classification system of hotels.

Training lab : A place fitted with specialised equipment to teach a specific skill.

Vocational training : To train for a skill related to a specific occupation in the service industry.

Appendix

Food and Accompaniments

Dish	Accompaniments	Cover
Hors d'oeuvre — *Appetizers*		
Caviar	Toast, butter or blinis (pancakes), finely chopped shallots, sieved hard boiled yolk and white of an egg	A fish knife on the right-hand side of the cover, a cold fish plate, a side plate and a cruet set *Silverware made from electroplated nickel silver (e.p.n.s) should not be used as a cover for this particular dish as it tarnishes the silverware.*
Tomato juice	Lemon wedges and Worcestershire sauce	A cruet set, a doily on a side plate, a swizzle stick or a teaspoon
Melon	Castor sugar and ground ginger	A dessert-spoon and fork, a cold half plate, a side plate and a side knife
Oysters	Chilli vinegar tobasco (capsico), lemon wedges, brown bread and butter	An oyster fork, a cayenne pepper mill, a soup plate or an oyster dish with crushed ice, a fingerbowl on an underliner, a side plate, a side knife and a cruet set
Pate de foie gras	Melba toast and butter	A cold fish plate, a side knife, a side plate and a cruet set
Smoked salmon	Lemon wedges, brown bread and butter	A fish knife and fork, a cold fish plate, a cayenne pepper mill, a cruet set, a side plate and a side knife
Shellfish cocktail	Lemon wedges, brown bread and butter	A cocktail dish on an underliner, a teaspoon, a side knife, a side plate and a cruet set

Dish	Accompaniments	Cover
Potage — *Soups*		
Minestrone	Grated Parmesan cheese, bread rolls and butter and macaroni as a garnish	A soup-spoon, a side knife, a side plate and a cruet set
French onion	Grated Parmesan cheese, grilled flute and a raw egg yolk (optional), bread rolls and butter	A soup-spoon, a side knife, a side plate and a cruet set
Cream soups	Bread rolls and butter	A soup-spoon, a side knife, a side plate and a cruet set
Tomato soup	Croutons and cream as garnish	A soup-spoon, a side knife, a side plate and a cruet set
Mushroom soup	Sliced mushrooms and cream as garnish	A soup-spoon, a side knife, a side plate and a cruet set
Asparagus soup	Asparagus and cream as garnish	A soup-spoon, a side knife, a side plate and a cruet set
Consomme Royal (Savoury cubes of egg custard) Consomme Celestine (Strips of savoury pancakes)	Takes its name from the garnish, bread rolls and butter	A dessert-spoon, a side knife, a side plate and a cruet set
Mulligatawny	Lemon wedges, rice as garnish and papad	A soup-spoon, a side knife, a side plate and a cruet set
Dal, mutton or paya shorba	Papad	A soup-spoon, a side plate and a cruet set
Farinaceous — *Pasta*		
Spaghetti Macaroni	Grated Parmesan cheese	A dessert fork on the right, a dessert-spoon on the left, a side plate and a cruet set
		The placement of dessert fork and spoon is interchanged because the spoon is used as a bowl. The spaghetti placed in the bowl of the spoon is picked up using the dessert fork. It is then turned and twisted around the prongs of the fork. This makes it easier to eat.
Poisson — *Fish*		
Crumb fried fish	Tartare sauce, lemon wedges, bread rolls and butter	A fish knife and fork, a side plate, a side knife and a cruet set
Batter fried fish	Tomato sauce, lemon wedges, bread rolls and butter	A fish knife and fork, a side plate, a side knife and a cruet set
Grilled fish	Melted butter, lemon wedges, bread rolls and butter	A fish knife and fork, a side plate, a side knife and a cruet set
Fish curry	White rice, pickle, papad and pickled onions	A dessert-spoon and fork, a side plate and a cruet set

Dish	*Accompaniments*	*Cover*
Viande — *Meat*		
Roast lamb	Mint sauce, roast gravy, bread rolls and butter	A large knife and fork, a side plate, a side knife and a cruet set
Roast mutton	Red currant jelly, onion sauce, roast gravy, bread rolls and butter	A large knife and fork, a side plate, a side knife and a cruet set
Roast beef	English mustard, horseradish sauce, Yorkshire pudding, roast gravy, bread rolls and butter	A large knife and fork, a side plate, a side knife and a cruet set
Roast pork	Sage and onion stuffing, apple sauce, roast gravy, bread rolls and butter	A large knife and fork, a side plate, a side knife and a cruet set
Mixed grill and steaks	English or French mustard, bread rolls and butter	A steak knife and fork, a side plate, a side knife and a cruet set
Mutton Rogan gosh	Indian bread *(naan, roti)* and/or rice, pickle, *papad* and pickled onions	A dessert-spoon and fork, a side knife, a side plate and a cruet set
Volaille — *Poultry*		
Roast chicken	Bread sauce, roast gravy, parsley and thyme stuffing, bread rolls and butter	A large knife and fork, a side plate, a side knife and a cruet set
Roast duck	Orange or apple sauce, roast gravy, sage and onion stuffing, bread rolls and butter	A large knife and fork, a side plate, side knife and a cruet set
Roast turkey	Cranberry sauce, chestnut puree, chipolatas, sage, onion and mince stuffing, roast gravy and chips	A large knife and fork, a side plate, a side knife and a cruet set
Chicken curry	Indian bread *(Naan, roti)*, and/or rice, pickle, *papad* and pickled onions	A dessert-spoon and fork, a side plate, a side knife and a cruet set
Tandoori chicken	*Tandoori* onion salad and mint *chutney*	An all purpose knife and fork, a side plate and a cruet set. (can also be eaten with fingers)

Dish	Accompaniments	Cover
Légumes — *Vegetables*		
Corn on the cob	Melted butter, lemon wedges and cream	Corn on the cob holders, a side plate, a side knife and a cruet set
Asparagus (Served hot)	Warm hollandaise sauce and melted butter	Asparagus tongs, a side knife and a side plate, a cruet set and fingerbowl *(an overturned fork under the right upper corner of the half plate to keep the tips of the asparagus in the sauce at all times)*
(Served cold)	Mayonnaise or vinaigrette	
Entrêmet — *Sweets*		
Hot or cold puddings or confectionery Souffle (Lemon, strawberry or chocolate)	Cream garnished with a lemon slice, strawberry fruit or chocolate chips respectively	A dessert-spoon and a fork and a dessert plate
Apple pie	Cream or ice-cream	A dessert-spoon and a fork and a dessert plate
Indian sweets		
Rasmalai or gulab jamoon		A dessert bowl and a teaspoon on an underliner
Ice-cream	Toppings as appropriate (nuts, sauce or choc chips)	A dessert bowl and a teaspoon on an underliner
Fromage — *Cheese*	Celery sticks in a glass jug with crushed ice, crackers, butter and mustard	A side plate, a side knife, a cruet set and a fingerbowl on an underliner
Dessert		
Fresh fruit and nuts	Castor sugar	A fruit knife and fork, a dessert plate, a side plate, grape scissors, nut crackers, a cruet set and a fingerbowl with cold water
Dessert is normally referred to in India as a sweet course, but in the French classical menu it means the service of fresh fruit and nuts.		
Café — *Coffee*		
Filter coffee, Cona coffee, Cappucino and South Indian coffee	White or brown sugar, milk or cream	Demitassé, a cup and saucer doily and a coffee spoon

References

1. Andrioli and Douglas., *Professional Food Service*, Heinemann Professional Publishing Limited, 1990.

2. Bamunnge and Karet., *Food and Beverage Service*, Macmillán Press Limited, Hampshire and London, 1989.

3. Collin., *Dictionary of Hotel, Tourism and Catering Management*, UBS Publishers, New Delhi, 1994.

4. Cousins, Foskett and Short., *Food and Beverage Management*, Longman Group Limited, 1995.

5. Davis and Stones., *Food and Beverage Management*, Butterworth Heinemann, Oxford, 1994.

6. Gullen and Rhodes., *Management in the Hotel and Catering Industry*, Batsford Limited, London, 1990.

7. Halliday and Hugh., *The Art and Science of Wine*, Mitchell Beazley, London, 1994.

8. Harris., *Profit Planning*, Butterworth Heinemann in association with Caterer and Hotel Keeper, Oxford, 1992.

9. Hayter., *Bar Service*, Macmillan Press Limited, Hampshire and London, 1996.

10. Hayter., *Careers, Training for Hotels, Catering and Tourism*, Butterworth Heinemann, Oxford, 1993.

11. Hayter., *Safety in Catering*, Berming Publication Limited, London, 1994.

12. Jones and Brehaunt., *Napkin Folding and Table Decoration*, Anees Publishing Limited, London, 1994.

13. Jones and Merricks., *The Management of Food Service Operations*, Cassel (Birtish Library Cataloguing in Publication Data), 1994.

14. Kinton and Cesarani., *Theory of Catering*, Educational, Academic and Medical Publishing, London, 1989.

15. Kotas and Davis., *Food and Beverage Control*, Chapman and Hall, 1990.

16. *Learning About Wines and Spirits*, Wine and Spirit Education Trust Limited, London.

17. Lillicrap and Cousins., *Food and Beverage Service*, Hodder and Stoughton (ELBS Edition), 1995.

18. Logie, Jayardena and Bowen., *The International Hospitality Business*, Hotel and Catering International Management Association.

19. Miller and Hayes., *Basic Food and Beverage Cost Control*, John Wiley and Sons Inc., U.S.A, 1994.

20. Montagne and Gottschalk., *Larousse Gastronomique : The World's Greatest Cookery Encyclopedia*, The Hamlyn Publishing Group Limited, 1988.

21. Ridgeway and Ridgeway., *The Catering Management Handbook*, Kogan Page, 1995.

22. Ryan., *Food and Beverage Service*, Macmillan Press Limited, Hampshire and London, 1989.

23. Waller., *Improving Food and Beverage*, in association with Caterer and Hotel Keeper, Butterworth Heinemann, Oxford, 1998.

Index